PREACHING THAT MATTERS

Preaching That Matters

The Bible and Our Lives

STEPHEN FARRIS

Westminster John Knox Press
Louisville, Kentucky

Book design by Jennifer K. Cox
Cover design by Alec Bartsch

First edition
Published by Westminster John Knox Press
Louisville, Kentucky

This book is printed on acid-free paper that meets the
American National Standards Institute Z39.48 standard. ∞

PRINTED IN THE UNITED STATES OF AMERICA
98 99 00 01 02 03 04 05 06 07 — 10 9 8 7 6 5 4 3 2 1

Library of Congress Cataloging-in-Publication Data

Farris, Stephen.
    Preaching that matters : the Bible and our lives / Stephen Farris.
        — 1st ed.
        p.   cm.
    Includes bibliographical references and index.
    ISBN 0–664–25759–3 (alk. paper)
    1. Bible—Homiletical use.   2. Analogy (Religion)   3. Preaching.
I. Title.
BS534.5.F37   1998
251—dc21   97–41406

Contents

Acknowledgments

There are many people who must be thanked not merely as a courtesy but rather from the bottom of my heart. Let me mention first my colleagues in the teaching of homiletics at the Toronto School of Theology, Professors Pamela Moeller, Art Van Seters, and Paul Scott Wilson. Art doubles as principal of my college in the TST and has always made a special effort to keep me from burying myself in college activities. Paul has been my mentor in the ways of publishing and a good friend. I owe thanks also to my patient and long-suffering teaching assistants, Brook Thelander, Soo Kwang Kwak, and Laura D. Alary successively. My own minister, Douglas Rollwage, is himself an excellent preacher and helps me pick up after my all too frequent computer disasters. I am also grateful to Jon L. Berquist, Catherine Carpenter, Esther Kolb, and the helpful staff of the Westminster John Knox Press.

Above all, I must record my love and gratitude for my dear wife, Patty, and my two sons, Allan and Daniel. I was going to write that they put up with me, but that is less than the truth. They love me and I am thankful.

The apostle Paul writes, "How shall they hear without a preacher?" (Rom. 10:14, KJV). But it would be equally proper to ask, "How can anyone preach without a hearer, in fact, many hearers?" I want therefore to record my thanks to and for those who have listened to me over the years. I have been blessed with the opportunity to preach in a wide variety of circumstances on five continents, but there are a number of groups with whom I have had a more long-lasting and official relationship. Let me name in particular, in chronological order:

The men of the Scott Mission, Toronto. If they were bored, they snoozed or they read their papers. If you caught their interest, they listened with a voracious curiosity.

The people of Knox Presbyterian Church, Bayfield, where I was student minister for three happy summers.

Montgomery and Smithers Presbyterian churches, West Virginia, where I had a fascinating intern year.

The members and adherents of Trinity Presbyterian Church, Amherstview, Ontario, where I was ordained to the work of preaching the gospel. Those were five happy years.

The faculty, staff, and above all, the students of Knox College, Toronto, where I teach preaching and, from time to time, try to preach myself.

The several churches where as interim moderator it has been my duty and joy to preach regularly: Unionville Presbyterian Church, Fallingbrook Presbyterian Church and Guildwood Community Presbyterian Church, both of Scarborough; St. Andrew's Presbyterian Church, Whitby; and St. Andrew's Church, Scarborough.

In thankfulness to God and in gratitude to these sisters and brothers I dedicate this book, such as it is,

To Those Who Have Listened

one

Preaching as Creative Analogy

THREE STRANGE CLAIMS

God speaks to us.

There is little point to preaching and certainly none to listening to preaching unless God speaks to us. But the church has always believed, and I myself believe with a whole though sometimes doubting heart, that God does speak to us.

> Long ago God spoke to our ancestors in many and various ways by the prophets, but in these last days he has spoken to us by a Son, whom he appointed heir of all things, through whom he also created the worlds. He is the reflection of God's glory and the exact imprint of God's very being, and he sustains all things by his powerful word. (Heb. 1:1–3)

Let us not forget for a minute how strange is this claim that we are addressed by God. On a clear moonless night in the autumn in my part of the world, away from the city's lights, one can, if one knows where to look, catch sight with even the naked eye of a faint hazy patch in the constellation Andromeda. That hazy patch grows remarkably even in a pair of binoculars; in an amateur telescope one may begin to catch sight of a spiral structure. The great telescopes show it to be a galaxy larger than our own Milky Way, a cloud of perhaps 1.4 billion stars. The light from that hazy patch began its journey to our eyes 2.2 million years ago, when our ancestors were clambering about the Olduvai Gorge. The Andromeda Galaxy is merely the largest member of the Local Group of galaxies. Even a relatively modest backyard telescope will show the observer galaxies forty million light-years distant. The Hubble Space Telescope and the great observatory telescopes show innumerable such galaxies *billions* of light-years distant!

I can grasp with only the edges of my mind and most certainly not with my entrails the enormity of such numbers. They freeze the entrails and

1

shrivel the mind, and they can shrivel the faith. I know, because they once shriveled my faith, but that is another story. We humans are by comparison but short-lived creatures and terribly small. The ancient poetry echoes with truth:

> When I look at your heavens, the work of your fingers,
> the moon and the stars that you have established;
> what are human beings that you are mindful of them,
> mortals that you care for them?
>
> (Psalm 8:3–4)

There is no way that we can prove that any God who created such things does care for us, does speak to us, or, in the words of the King James translation of this psalm, does "visit" us. We who believe can confess only that we sense a certain rightness in living as if such claims are true. With great audacity, then, we claim that "[God] has spoken to us by a Son . . . through whom he also created the worlds." We say, "In the beginning was the Word, and the Word was with God, and the Word was God. . . . All things came into being through him." We claim that the "Word became flesh . . . and we have seen his glory." These may seem commonplaces of Christian theology but they are, in truth, monstrously huge claims. A great awe is necessary here.[1]

How often this "speech" or "word" language recurs in our scriptures! This is at least in part because we sense that this particular part of the human experience, speech and word, is the most appropriate to apply to the God whose existence we claim. This God or, more properly, the relationship between this God and ourselves, can be represented only analogically; we can describe the indescribable only in terms of what we already know.[2] At least a limited anthropomorphism is inevitable in God talk. How could it be otherwise when we speak of a God who created both ourselves and the far-flung galaxies? The God-humanity relationship is not the same as the relationships that we know in our human interactions, but there is a certain likeness between our human interactions and our relationship with God. The human interaction that bears a particularly striking similarity to the God-human relationship is speech.[3] Speech and hearing, word and response, these are *like* what happens between God and humanity. We come to know this God and are convinced of this God's reality somewhat the way we know and are convinced of the reality of another person who addresses us. God's own Spirit impresses the reality of God and God's word on us: "When we cry, 'Abba! Father!' it is that very Spirit bearing witness with our spirit that we are children of God" (Rom. 8:15–16). We must not attempt to substitute, and indeed cannot substitute, any other testimony for the testimony that God's own Spirit provides.

We Christians may also bear testimony to this: that when we pay heed to the word that we believe is thus spoken to us, life begins to hang together for us; it makes a greater degree of sense than we would otherwise be able to perceive amid the chaos of life. This still falls far short of proof to the skeptic, but it is satisfying to the believer. This sense of satisfaction is also the inward work of the Holy Spirit.

We may, of course, be self-deceived. When we hear and respond to what we believe to be God's word, we may only be engaged in that common but not particularly respectable activity, talking to ourselves. This does not seem to us Christians to be the case; to us it seems rather that we are engaged in something like a conversation with God, a conversation in which God always has the first word. True conversation, meaningful speech and response, occurs with another. We Christians believe that the God who addresses us is genuinely such an Other. The God who speaks is not a projection into the heavens of our hopes and desires. Nor should that God be *identified* with the creation or any part of creation, though creation may, when viewed aright, point to the creator. Because God is Other and not merely some capital-letter version of ourselves, it is possible that there could be a relationship between God and ourselves. If there is no essential difference between God and creation, including ourselves, both the language of speech and the language of relationship are inappropriate and misleading. But we in the Christian church are convinced that God is genuinely an Other who desires to enter into relationship. God wishes to address us, to reveal God's own self to us. God has a word for us, both of total acceptance and complete demand, and wishes us to hear and trust that word. This book is based on that fundamental theological conviction.

God speaks to us through the Bible.

A second fundamental conviction is this: that God's speech comes to us through the story of Israel and of the life, death, and resurrection of Jesus Christ. This is not a claim that God speaks only through this story—surely God continues to speak "in many and various ways." It is to claim, however, that for us Christians this story is uniquely privileged in that by it we measure all other words and indeed actions to ascertain whether they might indeed come from God. "We can spot God's elusive presence only on the basis of precedent—previous disclosures of God that establish God's style and trace God's purpose."[4] A new word from God would cohere with the

Word we hear through that story. We probably could not recognize a word that does not so cohere as a word from God. This is not as limiting a statement as it first might appear. The story is not monolithic; it is so varied in its form, its circumstances of composition, and its content that it is not possible completely or confidently to predict what a word for our day will be. We can only say what it will sound like: it will sound like God's word to Israel or like God's Word in Jesus. One may therefore test claims that God is acting in certain ways or bears a certain character by reference to the experience of Israel and the person of Jesus Christ.

This story is, of course, the substance of our Bible.[5] We cannot prove that God speaks through the Bible any more than we can prove that God speaks at all. Once again we are dependent on the work of the Holy Spirit within us.[6] To this primary testimony may be added the subsidiary testimony of the church. The Bible is the church's canon, the body of sacred writings that we have used, not always successfully, to discover who we are and to order our common life and teaching. "Whatever else canon does, it serves to engage the two questions: Who am I (or we)? and, What are we to do? Canon functions, for the most part, to provide indications of the identity as well as the lifestyle of the ongoing community that reads it."[7]

The Bible, then, is the "identity story" of the church. (It is also in a sense the identity story of God, but that concept may be left aside for a moment.) It functions for that community the way that shared stories hold a family together. Consider what happens at a funeral when the identity of a family is shaken by the death of a matriarch or patriarch. After the service, which is arguably one of the least important events in the day, the family members get together, eat, drink, and remind one another of the stories that belong uniquely to their family. This is not all that different from church. We eat and drink together and we share our common stories. The preacher, as the church's licensed storyteller, does not go to the Bible as an independent inquirer, some sort of academic free agent, but as a representative of the church, indeed as a member of the family.[8] The preacher is sent by the congregation to wrestle deeply with these texts on its behalf. Such a person must take seriously the reality that the Bible is in this sense the church's book. Such a person must also take seriously the fact that the church has always claimed that God speaks through the Bible. No spurious claims of academic objectivity for the preacher! One may lecture on the Bible as literature or history or anything else; one may preach from it only as Word of God. The preacher, then, must go to the scripture expecting that God will speak through its words. We must not, however, allow the church's theological formulations to replace the inward testimony of the Spirit. Without that testimony, the individual is unlikely to be impressed by the affirmations of the church regarding the authority of scripture.

To call the Bible the church's book should not blind us to the fact that it too stands over against us in the church as an "Other." (The capitalization is a mistake, but let it stand for a minute.) It is not just the identity story of our church, but also the identity story of our God. It tells us who God is and what God has done. It is not our own; it comes to us as a voice from beyond.

In the first place, these are writings of a community or communities other than our own. The first part of our Bible consists of writings that in the present are often called Hebrew scriptures. The name is at least partially correct, since these writings were and are the sacred writ of communities that were not and are not Christian. It is of the first importance that we recognize that these people were different from us. The extent of the difference struck me most vividly in Hebrew class (thank God for Hebrew!) when I was learning the Hebrew verbal system. The Hebrews didn't have our complicated set of time relationships (no future perfect!), but they did have a special verbal stem for causing an action to happen, for an intensive form of the verb, and for an action that one does to oneself! Anybody who thought in these kinds of verb forms was different from me and people like me. I learned, and it was an important lesson, that I could not assume that I could understand automatically and without a great deal of thought what a text from these scriptures meant. It was for me an epiphany.

The Hebrew scriptures also served from the beginning as the scriptures of the early Christian church. (To call these writings only Hebrew scriptures as if they belonged solely to others and not to our own spiritual ancestors has about it the faint whiff of the heretic Marcion.) As such, they were for a time the church's only scriptures. After the church rejected Marcion, they became the inescapable first section of the church's Bible, the Old Testament. A second section of that Bible then came into being within communities that, like our own, claim Jesus Christ as Lord. But in our case, both Old and New are old indeed. They come to us from beyond a chasm of time and altered circumstance. The time is now approaching two millennia. The circumstances are too numerous even to list. They include changes that leave their mark in the writings themselves, the delay of the second coming of Jesus, once so imminently expected, and the inclusion of Gentiles in a once exclusively Jewish church. Many more come from the intervening centuries: the decline of one empire, the rise of several more, the establishment and decline of Christendom, an Enlightenment that declared humanity the measure of all things, a scientific method that seeks only proximate causes for events, Darwin and a theory of evolution that often denies a creator, Freud and a psychology that does the same. The list goes on.

There has been since the writing of even the New Testament a massive change in worldview. I still remember a professor in my seminary days summing up the change this way: "If engineers constructing a tunnel are blocked by a spring of water within the mountain they don't sit down and pray that God will take away the water." This would not seem to them a practical thing to do. By contrast, those in the early church, assuming they might have thought it important to build a tunnel, would have prayed. To them it would have seemed an entirely practical thing to do. Once again, it is differences of this sort that mean that we may not simply identify with the people in or behind the biblical text.

But the otherness of the Bible does not lie primarily in the time and circumstances of composition or in the flow of time between then and now. This otherness can easily be overstated. I will argue shortly that in certain key ways we are *similar* to the people who wrote, collected, preserved, and heeded the biblical texts in former times. The true distinction lies in the fact that we are here addressed by one who is an "Other." The genuine "Other," the one who alone deserves the capital letter, is God.

We say we hear in these writings—and this too is a surpassingly strange claim—a voice from beyond. In these writings, the church through the ages has come to sense the presence and the word of another. Beyond the communities, beyond the authors and all their human preoccupations, there is One who speaks. The preacher's task is to find faithful words for that voice from beyond.

God speaks to us through preaching.

There is a third theological conviction: that God speaks not only through the Bible but through contemporary preaching. Though some preaching is truly tedious and as meaningful and melodious as the quacking of a duck, we have all heard sermons in which we have sensed in that moment that God is speaking to us. Often such sermons are rhetorically skilled and exegetically sound, but sometimes a sermon that is, humanly speaking, wretched will speak God's word to us. This too is the inward testimony of the Holy Spirit. The church has also from time to time borne witness to the reality that God speaks even through preaching. "The preaching of the Word of God is the Word of God," declares the Second Helvetic Confession.[9]

We must not forget how strange is *this* claim also. Few of us preachers are intelligent beyond our peers. How many of us, after all, led our high school classes? Most of us don't work harder than our church members; they work full time and then put in many a long hour on top of that in the church. Even fewer of us are the most faithful and pious Christians in our congregations. Any experienced preacher knows that in the congregation there are some whose life bears a witness to the love of God that puts to shame both the words and the life of the preacher. These people are truly "saints," and yet they listen to us! But this is not the truly awesome strangeness of preaching. That strangeness lies in the notion that the God of the galaxies and the atoms speaks through weak and limited humans like *us!* No wonder Martin Luther, far from a shrinking violet of a person, said in his old age, "Though I am old and experienced in speaking, I tremble whenever I ascend the pulpit!"[10] We indeed ought to tremble before the chutzpah of the claim that God speaks through us. If it were not for the work of the Holy Spirit, the task would truly be beyond us—light-years beyond.

This, then, is the third strange claim: that we fallible humans can preach a word that comes from God, a word that truly matters. How we preachers can do so is, I trust, the substance of this book.

ANALOGY, THE MISSING LINK

Preaching may be recognized as the word of God when it coheres with the biblical witness. Normally this will mean that the sermon will grow from our interaction with a biblical text. There are, however, textual sermons that are profoundly unbiblical and nontextual sermons that are truly biblical. The criterion is not the form of the sermon but its coherence with the biblical witness. Coherence, it should be noted, is not a matter of otherness and dissimilarity but of likeness or similarity. Coherence is not, however, a matter of identification. The Word is always particular, as particular and concrete as a manger or a cross; it is addressed to specific people in specific times and circumstances. The times and circumstances of the biblical world are manifestly different from our own. Coherence therefore must lie in *similarity* and not in *identification*. If in preaching God speaks to us, it will in some ways be similar to the biblical witness. It will also be dissimilar in other respects, because of the passage of time and its attendant changes.

We need, then, in our preaching *a way of linking the world of the biblical text and the world in which we live and preach that affirms similarity but respects dissimilarity*. Analogy can be the link between worlds that we need.

Here is a working definition of analogy:

> To "draw an analogy" is to make a comparison between the similar features or attributes of two otherwise dissimilar things, so that the unknown, or less well known, is clarified by the known. Strictly speaking an analogy is predicated on the similarities which two things (concepts, entities, etc.) have in common.[11]

Notice in the definition both the words "similar" and "dissimilar." A good analogy depends on the former but respects the latter.

Nor does this definition involve an unusual meaning of the word. The various nonmathematical definitions of the word "analogy" in the *Oxford English Dictionary* stress only likeness, not identity, as, for example, "equivalency or likeness; resemblance of things with regard to some circumstances or effects." Let me borrow a pair of terms from the early christological controversies. Things related analogically are not *homoousion,* of the same substance, but *homoiousion,* of like substance.

Analogy is not only a likeness that respects unlikeness; it is also the means by which we integrate the old and the new. We cannot absorb the new unless we relate it to something we already know, at least in part. Faced with the new, we create bridges to the past. We say, "It's like the time when . . . " This enables us to appropriate the new and to deal with it. It is very difficult, perhaps impossible, for human beings genuinely to grasp anything totally new. From that which is only old there may not, on the other hand, be anything worth the trouble of grasping. The human person grasps best that which is at once both old and new. The Word of God, even in its preached form, is both old and new. It is old in that it inescapably depends on events long past—a band of slaves escaping from Egypt, exiles weeping by the waters of Babylon, a Roman cross on a hill outside Jerusalem. And yet it is also the word of a God who is an inveterate conversationalist, who continues to desire to speak to an assembled people even now, to address them in their very contemporary situation. Living preaching is new in that God speaks again through our preaching to the present situation of the church. Something old, something new—that's preaching. Analogy can link the old and the new when we preach.

Analogy, as its definition states, presupposes similarity. No analogy is possible where there is total dissimilarity. Nevertheless, analogy allows for and indeed demands that one recognize dissimilarity. Analogy in preaching is emphatically not the same as identification with the biblical world or characters in it. We cannot simply say, "We are the Pharisees," or "We are the children of Israel," or "the disciples." Complete dissimilarity, however, that is to say, the absence of any possibility of similarity, would prevent any word at all being spoken in the act of preaching. Complete similarity or identification, on the other hand, would prevent any new word from being spoken.

One fundamental similarity between the world of the Bible and our own world is the similarity of situation. The texts of the Bible address a community of people trying and often failing to live faithfully before God and with one another. The church today is likewise a community of people trying and often failing to live faithfully before God and with one another. That earlier community could live only by the grace of God; we too can live only by the grace of God. This fundamental similarity with the church today makes analogy possible. The fact that the culture in which preaching today takes place differs from the cultures of the biblical period in many and varied ways makes identification impossible and analogy necessary. There is a more significant similarity still, a theological one in the strict sense of the word. In fact, here we may speak of identity: by faith we are persuaded that the God who addresses us today is the same God who spoke through the prophets and through the Lord Jesus Christ. That God is faithful; there is a certain consistency in character in God's dealings with humanity. It is this faithfulness that makes analogical thinking both possible and necessary.

It is also true, of course, that the word comes to *humans* in both biblical times and our own. We may assume that we share with the inhabitants of the biblical world a common humanity. Once again, this common humanity must not be overstated. I believe homiletician David Buttrick is correct when he writes of a change in consciousness between the first-century world and ourselves.[12] We are still speaking only of similarity, not of identity.

A more theologically significant continuity lies in the fact that we interpret the Bible as *scripture,* within a *church.* (The skeptical and theologically uncommitted scholar producing work only for the professional guild of academics labors under *huge* interpretative disadvantages.) Biblical texts were composed, preserved, collected, and ordered into their present canonical position in order to meet some need or needs within the community of faith. To put it crudely, they scratched some itch. As a community of faith, those to whom we preach will have certain needs. It is possible that those needs will be analogous to the needs of the biblical community that caused the creation of the text being preached. There is therefore a possibility that there exists an analogy of need, or "itch," between the text's world and my own. This analogy can form the bridge between the text and ourselves over which the sermon can move. In this case the analogy is between the historical world "behind" the text and our world. Traditional historical-critical interpretation attempted with some degree of success to explore this historical world.

It is possible also that an analogy or several analogies can be discerned between the world "within" the text and our world. Newer forms of literary criticism can help the interpreter to discern the characters and to understand the movements of the world within the text. Texts have the capacity to be worlds in themselves and to suggest to us alternative and better worlds than our own, toward which we can live. This can happen if we explore the relationship between ourselves and the persons or groups within the text.

There are also forms of biblical study in which meaning is found "in front of" a text. Reader-response criticism, for example, seeks to understand the ways meaning can be created by the interaction of reader and text. The sermon is an event that likewise occurs "in front of" the text. Preaching requires a "listener response." Analogy can function as a means of shaping that response.

PREACHING AS ENCOUNTER

In all these uses of analogy the preacher is attempting to foster the creation of an *encounter* between text and contemporary listeners. I believe that the true "word of God" *for us* is the word that *happens* between God and the congregation as a result of this encounter between the biblical text and the people. Biblical scholar James Sanders claims:

> It is in this sense that one must insist that the Bible is not the Word of God. The Word is the point that is made in the conjunction of text and context, whether in antiquity or at any subsequent time.[13]

There are some problems with this formulation. The word "point" is feeble; the Word is not a conceptual summary of the text, as when we say, "The point is . . . " Moreover, the negative is overstated. While arguments about whether the Bible sitting on a shelf is the Word of God have always been fruitless, surely it can be said that the Bible functions instrumentally as the Word of God. It is through the encounter with *these* texts that the Word happens. But Sanders is, I believe, correct in what he affirms: the Word does happen now by means of the conjunction of text and context. This is how preaching can be, as the Heidelberg Catechism affirms, the present word of God.

That preaching is primarily encounter means that there is a difference between preaching, even biblical and expository preaching, and an exegetical lecture. It will not do to overstate the distinction; lectures about the Bible can be immensely stirring in a manner similar to that of an excellent sermon. I remember well many of my own professors of biblical studies with great fondness precisely because their academic treatments of the scriptures often became sermons. Indeed, if I am at all able to preach today it is because of their biblical teaching. Sermons, on the other hand, can be extraordinarily informative about the biblical text, even, from time to time, about its minutiae. The distinction between sermon and exegetical lecture is, however, real. An exegetical lecture is essentially descriptive. It explains the text by speaking intelligently, one hopes, about the text. For the most part, methods identical to or at least similar to those of the historian, the literary scholar, or the social anthropologist are used to explicate the text. The hope of the lecturer is that the listener will understand the text more profoundly as a result. With respect to the text, the lecturer hopes to uncover *meaning*. With respect to the listener, *understanding* is the aim of the lecturer.[14]

The preacher, on the other hand, prays that the sermon may become an encounter between the congregation and the living God. The aim of the preacher is not primarily to uncover meaning or to create understanding, but to hear and speak a word from God. In this encounter what may be communicated is not information about God but something of God's own self. The goal of the sermon is therefore not meaning as such, but *revelation*. The sermon can be, amazingly enough, a part of the process of revelation.

This insight makes one aware that the task of preaching is indeed different from the task of eliciting meaning from a text. Meaning can, in principle, be found in or created from any text and the processes of discovering meaning can be described, and in academic work usually are described, without any reference to God whatsoever. Revelation, on the other hand, cannot occur without the presence and activity of God. The word "revelation" contains within its definition in theology some sense of the self-disclosing activity of God. The concept of revelation is meaningless without a doctrine of the presence and work of God.

Once again, it will not do to overstate the distinction between revelation on the one hand and meaning and understanding on the other. Revelation can occur as one gains understanding. The relationship between the two is like the old overlapping circle Venn diagrams from our school days—the circles overlap, but they are nevertheless distinct. There is an old joke about two signs at a fork in the road to heaven. One points down one path and says "HEAVEN"; the other points the opposite way and says "LEC-TURES ABOUT HEAVEN." It is claimed that some of us professors of theology would take the second path! Preaching, however, must point down the first path.

But more can still be said. Christian theology has offered many different theories about the nature of revelation and many and varied descriptions of the manner in which it occurs. Christian theology in general, however, agrees that revelation occurs in a special manner or with a special degree of intensity in connection with *this* text, the Bible, in particular. In preaching, then, the aim is to allow God to speak through the text and the words of the preacher. Even the word "allow" may be too strong. Our God still speaks, and where there are people who will listen, nothing, not even the intention or the performance of the preacher, however sorry it may be, can finally stand in the way.

The language of revelation also presupposes another party in the process besides the God who reveals, namely, the one or ones to whom revelation comes. The Greek word *apokalupsis* lies behind our English word "revelation." It means "uncovering." "Uncovering" is a verbal noun; it describes the content of, or perhaps better the result of, a process or activity. In this case there is an uncovering to someone of something, or better, of someone, since that which is uncovered is at heart God's own self. Revelation is always "from" someone "to" someone.

There are several consequences of this approach. First, the purposes of preaching will be similar to the purposes of revelation itself. I take those purposes first to be the disclosure of God's own self in the face of Jesus Christ through the power of the Holy Spirit. That God is love and justice, mercy and righteousness. Second, with respect to the listeners the goal is once again not an increase in understanding but those human responses to God of which the scripture speaks so often, trust and obedience.[15] Trust and obedience together make up the reality of love.

To put it crudely, the desire of the preacher is that people will "get saved." This is a blunter and less elegant way of referring to that phenomenon of a consciousness of "being saved in the world" of which David Buttrick writes.[16] An older preacher once told me about a guide taking a group of American tourists through Westminster Abbey. The guide waxed eloquent on the architectural majesty of the Abbey and on the glories of the dead buried within its precincts. Finally one of the tourists asked, "But has anybody been saved here recently?" "Madam," the guide responded with hauteur, "this is not a Salvation Army citadel." The preacher claimed sympathy with the American tourist, and rightly so. The purpose of a church, even a Gothic treasure like Westminster Abbey, has more to do with being saved than it has to do with architectural splendor or dead poets.

Understanding is always a good thing in itself, as is also architectural beauty. One hopes (vainly!) that every church will be architecturally beautiful and that every sermon will increase understanding. With respect to preaching, understanding is, however, a means to an end or the by-product of an end, not the end itself. Trust, obedience, love, salvation, these are various ways of speaking of the complex reality that is actually preaching's end.

I used to say to my students, "Don't leave your text in the first century." That is still good advice, but is no longer wholly relevant to the point at issue. In my own seminary education there was a concentration on studies that located the meaning of the text in the intention of the author or in the historical circumstances behind the text.[17] Here the value of the text lay in the fact that it provided clues to what really mattered, either the historical event or the intention of the author. Here meaning lies "behind" the text. Revelation too, in this view, lies behind the text, once again with the "mighty acts of God" to which the text bears witness or in the inspiration of the author. (I do not wish to suggest, even for a moment, that there was not a great deal of truth to this view of scripture. If there are or were no "mighty acts of God," our faith is a useless, fraudulent thing.) My advice supposed, only partially correctly, that present-day students in my school were being taught the same sorts of exegesis that I was taught. In the present time, however, there are methods of study that locate meaning "in" the text (various forms of literary or narrative criticism) or "in front of" the text (reader-response criticism). Such approaches do not leave the text in the first or any other biblical century. The point at issue here is not a question of when revelation occurs but of meaning/understanding on the one hand versus revelation on the other.

Another point ought to be made here. The search for meaning is a search for a meaning to be found in relation to the text. Revelation, on the other hand, occurs with respect to God. It also means that it is not the first and only responsibility of the preacher to explain the content of a particular biblical text. To a certain point the argument of homiletician David Buttrick and theologian Edward Farley, that it is our task to preach the gospel rather than to preach the text, is compelling.[18] As one trained in technical biblical studies and an inheritor of a tradition of text-centered preaching, I have always been tempted to proclaim that the only good sermon is a sermon that grows out of and explains a specific text. Any such claim is, I have come to realize, an overstatement. There have been more great sermons than I would care to acknowledge that have effectively proclaimed both the total acceptance of God in Christ and God's total demand for repentance, and which do not grow from the study of a particular text. No, a greater understanding of the text, if that occurs, is a happy by-product of preaching. The goal itself is a clearer sense of the nature of the relationship of the person, the church, or the world to God. That is to say, there will, one hopes, be a deeper involvement between the person or the people and God as a result of the sermon. From time to time a listener will hang behind the line of exiting worshipers shyly to say how deeply the sermon has spoken to her or to him. It is precisely the desire to speak of this involvement with God that causes the listener to hang behind to speak to the preacher. The sermon, then, should be centered on the work of God rather than merely on the words of the text. The ultimate subject of every Christian sermon ought to be the presence of God among us in Christ Jesus. Such a sermon will be profoundly biblical although not necessarily profoundly textual.

Why, then, should the preacher care about a particular text at all? Perhaps this concern for particular texts that has so marked much great preaching also grows from the nature of revelation. Revelation is distressingly particular. It occurs to particular people in particular places. It is linked to the history of a particular people and shines forth in a particular face, marked with the imprint of very particular and very sharp Palestinian thorns. Revelation is not a matter of communicating a few general concepts to enlighten the collective mind of humanity. It is the involvement of a scandalously particular God with a particular people. Wrestling homiletically with particular texts forces us, whose education has often prepared us to think primarily in vague generalities, to come face to face with this particularity. We may limp into the pulpit from the encounter, but it will have been an encounter with the God of Israel and of Jesus Christ and not the God of the philosophers that has bruised us.

This leads us to another point. The human mind, perhaps particularly the homiletical mind, is an incorrigible factory of idols. The function of the biblical text is to ensure that the God whose presence we proclaim is not merely an idol of our own creation but rather the God and Father of our Lord Jesus Christ. Paradoxically, while we preach God in Christ rather than the text itself, it will most often be the words of the text that will enable us to speak rightly of the presence of God. While there have been many great and profoundly biblical though nontextual sermons, there have been far more such sermons that have been windy expositions of the preacher's own spiritual notions. A sermon that proclaims the gospel contained in the Christian Bible but does so apart from any particular text will almost invariably turn out to be a sermon that could have been derived from a particular text or texts. This is that "coherence" with the biblical word of which I have spoken earlier. I believe that we will always intend to preach the gospel of God in Christ but it will most frequently be a gospel preached from texts. Preaching from texts will be the meat and potatoes or pasta or rice of effective preaching. That is to say, it will be the staple of a healthy homiletical diet. In this work I shall attempt to suggest a method that can help make such textual preaching richly biblical. I do *not* suggest that it is the only proper method of preaching.

But more needs to be said: The preacher ought to have a little humility about his or her own work. This goes double for the one who, like me, presumes to write a book about preaching methodology. The "marrow" of preaching is always something beyond our control. The life-giving power in preaching comes not from the preacher's skill or eloquence and most certainly not from her or his mastery of homiletical method. It comes from God. That is to say, not only the subject matter of Christian preaching is God's; the power of preaching is also God's. That, of course, is a pious statement. (It is odd how we preachers and theologians cringe from the very adjective "pious.") It is, like the best pious statements, also realistic. There is a story about the great Baptist preacher of the nineteenth century, C. H. Spurgeon. Spurgeon, it is known, was converted on hearing the sermon of a preacher so incompetent that he could do little more than repeat his text over and over and over again. The power in that sermon most definitely did not belong to the preacher!

Modern preachers often experience something of the same reality. I have sometimes encountered an odd phenomenon: when I have preached a sermon of which I am very proud, with excellent exegesis, intelligent structure and movement, and good flow of language, people at the door are merely—polite. Sometimes, on the other hand, I preach so badly that if I were a canary they would throw a blanket over my cage.[19] How often it is precisely on such a Sunday that some person or persons have hung behind in the retreating line of worshipers shyly to tell me some story of their life and say how deeply the sermon has affected them. All this is not an argument for shoddy or incompetent preaching. Any work for God, including preaching, must be done to the very best of our abilities: "Thou shalt not make a sacrifice that costs thee little!" I believe with my whole heart that God will honor the efforts of those who use the best of their human gifts in the preaching task. Indeed I do not believe that these moments of grace, for both listener and preacher, will occur very often if the preacher does not put the very best efforts possible into the preaching task. It is, rather, merely to say that the power in preaching is not ours, and it is beyond our control.

It is, perhaps, sometimes the case that an appeal to the work of the Spirit to explain the process of revelation that can occur in the preaching event may be merely a way of avoiding the hard human work that is required to understand the process of interpretation. This hard human work is, of course, the art or science of hermeneutics. Hermeneutics seeks to understand the principles and processes behind this work of interpretation. Interpretation is not, of course, confined to the Bible and is not practiced by Christians alone. There is what is often called general hermeneutics. Such hermeneutics can be laid out without appeal to the work of the Spirit of God. The "regional" hermeneutics that belongs to the preaching task may not leave out that work, however. The chief interpreter in preaching is never the preacher but always the Holy Spirit. The wind of the Spirit blows where it will in preaching. The best any author of homiletical texts can do is to give advice about the best way to trim the sails.

If preaching is part of revelation, it should consciously cohere in its method with what we believe about the nature of revelation. The preacher may well be wise to consider preaching, like revelation, as a conversation in which there are two parties. The preacher will study the nature of the people who sit in the pew and the society in which they live as carefully as she does the texts or the theological tradition. The old saw attributed to Karl Barth remains valid: "The Bible in one hand and the newspaper in the other."[20]

As we have seen, preaching involves the person and the believing community and their contemporary life in a way that an exegetical lecture does not. Furthermore this involvement is precisely on the spiritual and practical level. It issues in trust, obedience, and, in the end, love. Compare with the task of preaching the task of literary interpretation as stated by narrative critic Mark Allan Powell in the following quotation:

> Readers are also led by stories to make such identifications with real people in the real world. Harriet Beecher Stowe's novel *Uncle Tom's Cabin* aroused the sympathy of readers not only for the characters in the story but also for African-American people in general. . . . Narrative critics would regard such considerations as extraneous to the task of interpreting a text as *literature*.[21]

I suspect that a person who reads *Uncle Tom's Cabin* who does *not* come away with a sympathy for "African-American people" and a loathing for the historical institution of slavery has missed the point of the book. That, however, is up to the literary critics to debate. Preaching will have none of such detached approaches to interpretation. A case can be made that several different forms of biblical interpretation are especially useful for preaching; I do not propose to judge between their claims at the moment. I only say that biblical interpretation that leads to good preaching will always be *involved*.

It is precisely the effect of the text on the listener that is at issue in preaching, for it is this effect that may very well be the word of God that preaching seeks to speak. The preacher knows that if his words do not in some way move the congregation to a more grateful sense of God's love and a determination more completely to obey God's will, something has gone profoundly wrong. But sometimes, perhaps even often, it does go right. Surprisingly often sermons that wrestle with texts with a view to finding through those texts the voice of God will allow our people to hear that voice. And when that happens the people will be grateful far beyond our deserving. My intention in this book is to help the reader use analogy to shape sermons that will allow this wonderful thing to happen.

The Word, then, is in the encounter. The preacher cannot create the encounter between God and people; the living God is beyond our homiletical manipulation! We who ascend the pulpit must never forget that the wind of the Spirit always blows where it wills. The preacher can only create an encounter between text and people and trust that in that lesser encounter with the text there will be the greater encounter with the God to whom the text bears witness.

Any method that brings text and people together might function this way. My claim here is simply that the use of analogy can be a particularly powerful and effective means of facilitating this encounter. But let us not get too cocky about our abilities. Listen to the warning from David Buttrick:

> Analogy is the language of faith. Yet analogy in and of itself is insufficient. Analogy draws the mystery of God into the human world but in so doing it can easily domesticate God and make the gospel trivial. . . . The obvious danger in analogy is that it can paint our image on the face of God and scale down God's revelation to our conventional wisdom.[22]

It should be clear by now that I am not merely speaking of occasional uses of contemporary language to enliven the description of biblical persons and situations. A New York area preacher might say of an arbitrary and tyrannical King Herod in the Bible, "He was like a first-century George

Steinbrenner, only he didn't just fire managers—he executed sons." That is lively description, frosting on the homiletical cake, but little more. Rather, we are looking for more fundamental similarities and dissimilarities between worlds. Analogy, as used in this book, is a hermeneutical principle that links us to the biblical world and can give shape to our sermons as a whole. It's not the frosting on the cake but, rather, the recipe for the cake itself.

The use of analogy means a grasping of patterns of similarity between texts in the scripture and Christian experience today. It is an act of the imagination; one cannot legislate the use of analogy, although I shall suggest certain guidelines for its use. The use of analogy should be, strictly speaking, theological. The focus of the preacher should not be on insignificant correspondences of situation; one must seek to discern the outlines of God's action in text and world.

ANALOGY IN BIBLE AND PREACHING

The use of analogy to move from the world of the text to the world of the sermon has been part of the stock-in-trade of great preachers for many centuries. A particularly memorable example for me comes from Martin Luther King Jr.'s last sermon. The night before he died, he spoke in a Memphis church. Moving from an Old Testament story to the lives of his listeners, he claimed that he had been to the mountaintop, seen into the promised land, and that, though he might not get there, the people most certainly would do so.[23]

It is impossible to miss the fundamental analogy here: African Americans are in some sense similar to the children of Israel. Dr. King himself fills for them something of the role of Moses. Above all, one can trust that God will act in ways similar to his actions in the exodus. The people will reach the Promised Land. Behind this one memorable line is a history of analogical interpretation and preaching. Not one of us would doubt its effectiveness.

Nor is this method of interpretation of the Bible the property of one rhetorical genius. Literary critic Stanley Fish argues that interpretation of texts is done within what he calls "interpretative communities."[24] Behind this memorable speech there exists an interpretative community, a tradition of African American preaching that sees a fundamental analogy between the events and characters of the biblical period, particularly the exodus, and the struggle of the African American people in our country. This interpretative community thought analogically. So it is quite natural that on the wall of the motel where Dr. King was slain the next day, there was placed by the Southern Christian Leadership Conference a plaque that quotes Genesis 37:19–20:

> Here comes this dreamer. Come now, let us kill him . . . and we shall see what will become of his dreams.

Here the analogical link is from the biblical figure of Joseph to King, but once again the way of thinking about and using scripture is manifestly the same. So effective is this mode of thinking that the analogy does not need fully to be spelled out. A community versed in the sacred story takes the point.[25] The reference to one point in the Joseph story reminds the reader of the rest of the story. You cannot kill the dream by slaying the dreamer, for this dream, like Joseph's dream, comes from God and cannot in the end be defeated.

This mode of thinking was not invented in the African American community, however; it is present in the Bible itself. It is usually called typology, but typology is actually a form of analogical thinking. Gerhard von Rad, in his classic essay "Typological Interpretation of the Old Testament," repeatedly insists that such interpretation is a form of analogical thinking.[26] So Deutero-Isaiah, Isaiah 40—55, sees an analogical relationship between the exodus and the "new thing" that God will do for the oppressed exiles in Babylon. For Hosea the time in the wilderness will be repeated when the faithful God of Israel again deals graciously with a faithless people (Hosea 11). The brazen serpent that brings healing to stricken Israelites is a type of the salvation brought by the lifting up of Jesus on the cross (Num. 21:4–9; John 3:14). Christians are saved through baptism as Noah and his family were saved through the flood (1 Peter 3:20–21). Christians also pass through baptism as the Israelites passed through the sea, are fed as the Israelites were fed with manna, and drink from Christ as the Israelites drank from the rock (1 Cor. 10:1–5).[27] Moreover large stretches of the New Testament are composed in such a way that the alert reader will recognize that an Old Testament figure or event makes clear the significance of what is being described in the New.[28]

Early Christian preaching also made use of analogy. The oldest Christian sermon outside the Bible is the so-called *Second Letter of Clement*. Scholars have long recognized that this work is not an epistle at all, but rather a homily. It is a rather tedious moralistic sermon, notable only for its antiquity. Boring preaching is not a twentieth-century phenomenon alone! The preacher does, however, link text and contemporary church analogically. The barren woman of Isaiah 54:1, now made fertile by the grace of

God, becomes for the preacher a figure of the church, once barren but now fertile with converts.[29]

A far more interesting, though sadly anti-Judaic, early sermon is the second-century Paschal Homily of Melito of Sardis. This homily has certain characteristics of a narrative sermon. It links by means of analogy in a poetic and compelling manner the work of God for Israel in the exodus and the work of Christ for the church in his passion and resurrection.

> Just so also the mystery of the Lord
> having been prefigured well in advance
> and having been seen through a model,
> is today believed in now that it is fulfilled,
> though considered new by men.
> For the mystery of the Lord is new and old:
> old according to the law
> but new with reference to the grace.[30]

Note the combination of old and new!

Later preachers also made use of this principle. Calvin's careful historical exegesis had a particular homiletical goal. He carefully laid out the historical circumstances of his biblical texts so that his audience could apply the word appropriately to the sixteenth century:

One of the benefits derived from historical interpretation is clarity regarding how a passage is to be applied to one's own day. If one is to know how to apply scripture, one must know something of the time and circumstances of its composition. . . . There is a danger of drawing the wrong analogy if the historical setting is disregarded.[31]

In Calvin's sermons the text was not simply expounded; it was applied to those persons or groups to whom it was analogically appropriate.[32]

Mark Ellingsen, whose homiletical theory is in a number of respects similar to my own, points out that Luther could use this sort of analogical linking in a particularly winning manner. In a famous Christmas sermon, Luther describes vividly the difficulties Mary and Joseph endured in Bethlehem. Then he moves to our world: "If I had been there I would have given up my room! Oh? Just as you always have, whenever Christ comes to you in your neighbour? Of course you would not have given up your room!"[33] Ellingsen finds examples of such movement from biblical texts to contemporary listeners in preachers, speakers, and writers as diverse as John Wesley, Abraham Lincoln (the Second Inaugural Address), and Albert Schweitzer.[34]

Contemporary preachers do the same. Here are only a few of many possible examples. "Have you ever heard John preach?" asks Fred Craddock repeatedly in a sermon of that name.[35] Of course it's possible to hear John the Baptist preach because we can share the same experiences of repentance and forgiveness that John's first listeners experienced.

> Did you ever hear John preach? If you haven't you will. Because the only way to Nazareth is through the desert. Well, that's not really true. You can get to Nazareth without going through the desert. But you won't find Jesus.

David Buttrick also employs analogy: "God will provide, cries Abraham. . . . Well, here we are stumbling down a stone-hill Calvary into the twentieth century. We are free to trust God for God will provide."[36] Elizabeth Achtemeier uses analogy in "Of Children and Streets and the Kingdom."[37] In that sermon she works out at great length both the dissimilarities and the similarities between the people of the prophet Zechariah's times and our own. The list could be prolonged indefinitely.

South African preacher Allan Boesak uses analogy with immense power. In "The Finger of God," Boesak describes vividly the mighty acts performed by Moses and Pharaoh's stubborn refusal to see in them "the finger of God."[38] He reminds the listener of the vision of the white horse bearing a rider named "Faithful and True" that is granted to the "banned" John on the island of Patmos. This rider will most certainly triumph over the emperor! But "the pharaoh, the baals, the emperor, the powers of to-day—they all see it eventually, the finger of God." The analogy here is clear; the powers of today are similar to Pharaoh and to the emperor in the biblical text. The other side of the analogy is also clear. Oppressed South Africans are like those for whom God has acted in the past—the children of Israel and the witness John!

I would go so far as to say that the large majority of preachers, whatever their race, gender, or theological tradition, make use of analogy in their sermons, though often on an unconscious and unexamined level.

A key biblical scholar, James A. Sanders, urges us to make conscious and explicit use of analogy as an interpretative principle. For Sanders it is the use of what he calls "dynamic analogy" that allows us to read the ancient texts of scripture as a word for us today.

> To attempt to make the same points again today one must employ the basic rule of dynamic analogy. If a prophet challenged ancient Israel, or if Jesus challenged his own Jewish, responsible contemporaries, then a prophetic reading of the Bible today should challenge those dynamically equivalent to those challenged in the text. . . . Dynamic analogy also means that one reads

the text for oneself and not only for others. It should not be read to identify false prophets or Pharisees with another group or someone else, but with one's own group and with oneself, in order to perceive the right text in the right context.[39]

The purpose of this book is to help the preacher recognize and use these "dynamic" analogies.

Some homileticians have also explicitly advocated the use of analogy. Elizabeth Achtemeier urges the preacher to move by way of analogy from the setting in life of the text, that is, the world behind the text, to our own setting in life.[40] Mark Ellingsen, by contrast, turns from the historical context to the literary, from the world behind the text to the world within the text. He searches for analogies "between a text's literary context and our contemporary situation."[41] He explicitly rejects consideration of the text's historical context. In this book, however, I will attempt to recognize and make use of both the historical and the literary contexts of the texts.

ANALOGICAL PREACHING
AND THE POWER OF IDEAS

There has been in contemporary homiletics a commitment to narrative theology and a reaction against sterile rationalist preaching that reduces lively stories, hymns, proverbs, and everything else to a proposition. Fred Craddock called that sort of preaching "boiling down a cup of coffee and preaching on the stain in the bottom of the cup"! I share both the commitment and the reaction. But neither ought to lead us to a denigration of ideas.[42] I intend to honor not only the narrative but the nonnarrative portions of scriptures. I also intend to recognize the *ideas,* biblical concepts, that are conveyed within narrative and nonnarrative texts alike.

It is true that contemporary homiletics tends to be concerned more with creating an experience than with persuading the congregation to accept an argument.[43] Preachers want the congregation to experience the presence of God rather than to accept a series of propositions about God. Many homileticians have consequently urged the preacher to pay attention to the form of the biblical text and not to seek to force all biblical texts into the mode of rational exposition. Such exposition reduced poetry and parable and praise and a flock of other forms to a series of rationally ordered propositions, often the much-derided "three points and a poem." Such sermons often sucked the life out of the text.

In reaction against such sterile preaching, which might touch the head but never got very near the heart, some homiletical theorists have begun to treat the very notion "idea" as a four-letter word. But an honest description of the form of a good deal of biblical literature might well be "rational exposition," cast often in a rather discursive mode. Scholars have also discovered that parts of the Bible are cast in the form of rational argument, using the kind of rhetoric a person in the ancient world might hear, for example, in a law court or an assembly.[44] It actually often appears as if the author wanted to persuade the listener to accept certain ideas about God! Even in those parts of the Bible that are cast in forms other than rational argument, and those parts are extensive, ideas are omnipresent.

It is true that ideas about God can never be a satisfactory substitute for an experience of God. But it seems to be an enduring human characteristic that we human beings want to relate those experiences to one another and to evaluate and order them, using our human capacity for rational thought. One wonders whether the divorce between experience and idea that may inadvertently be engendered by some preaching is not an expression of an unhealthy dualism. Most people, after all, possess both a heart and a head in the same body, and neither ought to be denied. Preaching must appeal to both heart and head. The truth is that the Bible is full of ideas about God and humanity and often tries to put those ideas into a coherent and reasonable order. The Bible is concerned with ideas; so should the preacher be. To preach biblically means to be concerned with ideas and to want to communicate them. Such preaching is desperately needed in churches, where many of the people have only the shakiest grasp of some of the *key ideas* of the Christian faith. To ignore this state, to preach only to create an experience, is to do no good service to the church.

Biblical ideas do not float in lonely splendor in a world high above the muck of life. People come to them as a result of their experience of God, of others, of life itself. Ideas then have an effect on the lives of genuine people. The effect may be glorious or disastrous: Consider the effects of the ideas that "all people are created equal" and "Jews are an inferior race." Ideas matter—they can kill or bring to life. They are far too powerful to ignore! So we will try to recognize ideas and, where it is due, honor them. We will also, therefore, look for analogies in connection with ideas. It may be, for example, that the way a person or group in the Bible came to grasp an idea will be analogous to something in our world. It may likewise be that the consequences of living by an idea in the biblical world will be similar to something that can also happen in our own world. We will search our texts not for naked ideas, but for ideas incarnate in human experience, and seek analogies to them in our world. It may be that analogical preaching can help us deal with heart and head together.

What we have stated here suggests an attitude about preaching. It also suggests some of the preliminary work that must be done by a preacher, no matter what form or style the preacher may adopt for the sermon. There is no "one size fits all" style of preaching—nor is the way of preaching I advocate here that nonexistent "one size." I do suggest, however, that there is very frequently a fundamental analogy between Bible and contemporary world that gives life to sermons of vastly different styles. Behind many sermons, delivered in a wide range of preaching styles, there is a spoken or unspoken analogy between something in or behind the text and something in the contemporary world. Preachers of biblical texts must always make or suggest connections of relevance to the lives of their hearers. Very often these connections are created by means of analogy. The real question is not whether we will use analogies between the biblical world and our own but whether we will use compelling and appropriate ones and whether we will do so consciously or unconsciously.

We can, if we so desire, make use of analogy quite consciously and deliberately to shape the sermon. The sermon itself may justifiably become an exploration of analogies, successively "trying out" the various analogical possibilities in the text. This method can produce both engagement with and movement through the text. Where the biblical text is a narrative, it may be combined easily with a narrative approach, but the power of analogy is not confined to narrative texts.

This way of looking at preaching demands that the preacher be familiar with both the world of the text and the contemporary world. Without this double-sided familiarity analogies may well be mistaken and far-fetched. They could then be unpersuasive or—and this would be worse—wrongly persuasive. No method of interpretation and no homiletical style is safe from misuse. We turn now to exegesis, or to put it in nontechnical language, to ways of increasing our familiarity with ourselves, the world in which we preach, and the biblical text.

two

This Side
of the Analogy

It is not enough merely to study carefully the ancient texts of the scriptures. The analogical preacher must know at least something about the contemporary world. We noted in chapter 1 the old saying, attributed to Karl Barth, that the preacher must prepare for the sermon with the Bible in one hand and the newspaper in the other. Barth himself did not always preach this way. "All honor to relevance, but pastors should be good marksmen who lift their guns beyond the hills of relevance."[1]

The reason for Barth's objection to the supremacy of relevance is worthy of consideration, not for reasons of academic archaeology, but because it may clarify what is meant here by analogy. The use of analogy involves the perception of a "point of contact" between the text and our world. As part of his reaction against nineteenth-century liberal theology Barth objected vociferously to any notion of a "point of contact" between God and humanity save the point of contact that *God* supplies, the Word made flesh in Jesus Christ. Specifically, he objected to any notion of an "analogy of being" between God and ourselves, that God's nature and our fallen nature are somehow analogous enough that one can reason upward, as it were, from humanity to God. Even though humanity is created in God's image, God is not like us; God is "totally other." The starting place for theology can never be fallen humanity's religiousness; that is as likely to reflect the demonic as the divine. The starting place for theology must be the Word God provides, the Word made flesh in Jesus Christ, to which the written word bears witness. This is also true for preaching, for, according to Barth, "theology as a church discipline ought in all its branches to be nothing other than sermon preparation."[2] The preacher's task, then, is not to speak wisely from her or his own wisdom about the contemporary world, but to be an obedient servant of the Word.

Barth's theology has certain very specific homiletical consequences. One ought not, for example, to have an introduction, not simply because introductions are often boring, tangential, or trivial, but because they usually attempt to create some point of contact between the Word and the world. For similar reasons, one ought not to use conclusions. These provide a "summing up" which often is an attempt by the preacher to add his or her own word to the sovereign Word. The preacher is not to substitute for that Word her own reflections on culture or social issues. Perhaps, given all these objections, one ought not to attempt an exegesis of the situation and one ought not to preach analogically. You, as reader, will be ready for the "But" by this point! Even Barth's theology allows for the possibility of a different sort of analogy, however—the analogy of relationship or analogy of grace. That is to say that some human relationships are analogous to the relationship between God and humanity. Nevertheless, the use of analogy I am advocating here does not rest on a notion of an analogy either of being or of grace, but rather of situation. The analogy at work, and thus the "point of contact," is not an analogy between humanity and God either in nature or relationship, but between people in biblical times, on the one hand, and in our time, on the other. Analogy rests on a bedrock of similarity, and the key similarity, once again, is that we, like the folk of the Bible, are those who are addressed by God.

If it is not true that God has addressed humanity, and if it is not likewise true that God continues to address humanity, all preaching is a useless and windy effort, and I for one would choose to seek a more socially useful job like flipping hamburgers in a fast-food joint! But I am persuaded, and far more important the church through the ages has been persuaded, that God *does* address us as God in former times addressed Israel and the church. There is an analogy, indeed in this instance an identity of situation, between Israel, early church, and ourselves: we are those who are addressed by the Word of God.

If all this is substantially true, and the objection to such a theological position would not come from Karl Barth, then surely it is right to explore the possibility of analogies between the world of the text and our world. If this is the case, it is also necessary to carry out an exegesis of the preaching situation. Now Barth is quite correct that preachers who foist on their congregations their own windy observations on contemporary culture are misusing the pulpit. But surely an exegesis of the contemporary situation carried out in obedience to the word of God will look different from one carried out merely according to contemporary forms of social analysis. The exegesis of the situation must be biblical and theological; it must be carried out in obedience to the word of God and under the guidance of the Holy Spirit insofar as this is possible. To the objection that such an exegesis will inevitably be flawed and that it will most certainly speak not God's word alone but the preacher's word also, I can only say, "What else is new?" If we Christians are not to do a thing because it will inevitably be flawed, we will necessarily do nothing at all! Barth himself performed a theological and biblical exegesis of his own contemporary situation in Germany in the early 1930s. This exegesis of the situation led to the magnificent statement of theological repudiation of Hitler and Nazism, the Barmen Declaration.

If all this is true, it is the preacher's heavy responsibility to know not only the scripture but also the culture, the situation, and the self. This is, of course, an utterly impossible task! But do we not preach that God, if trusted, can help us to do what at first seems impossible? In this, as in most things, the preacher should follow Luther's words "Sin boldly, but believe and rejoice in Christ even more boldly."[3]

KNOW THE CULTURE

It is, sadly, the case that many of us ministers are not at all familiar with the culture in which we live. We prefer to live, some of us, in our own safe little religious enclaves, tended by and tending to a shrinking minority of the like-minded who have their own forms of speech and their own ways of doing things. There is a story, probably apocryphal, about a minister preaching a terminally sappy nature sermon one spring:

> Dear friends, at this lovely time of year God makes the world to burst with signs of love. Each shoot of grass, each tender new flower, is a personal sign of divine love for you. It is as if God points to each new shoot of life and says, "This bud's for you."

That is a minister who is out of touch with popular culture! But we ought to laugh with more than a trace of discomfort. Dominant Western culture in its decay has fertilized a garden of subcultures. How can any of us know that we are not saying something that inadvertently will sound as stupid in some setting as "This bud's for you"?

After all, the same word means different things in different subcultures. Not too long ago I lunched with a number of our second-career students. It happened that they all, like me, had early-adolescent children. Conversation passed, as it often seems to under such circumstances, to the peculiarities of speech of our teenagers. We puzzled for a considerable time over the meaning of the verb "bites." That is a verb that I use from time to time in a positive sense; I might say to a student preacher, "When you are specific about our social sins, that sermon really bites!" We eventually figured out that a comment "That sermon really bites!" is something our children might well say . . . but not exactly as a compliment! The truth is that we live in a culture of subcultures. Each of those subcultures has its own patterns, its own customs, and, above all, its own particularities of image, ideas, and language. Cross-cultural communication is not merely a problem for missionaries who travel to different lands—it is a problem within churches and, yes, within families. How can we know even superficially the particular subcultures in which so many of our people live?

Even if we were to speak not simply of subcultures but of the mass culture of our society, the problem remains severe. By culture I mean at this point particularly the web of stories and images that exists in the minds of a large percentage of the population. It is this web of images that is useful in preaching. Indeed, it is hard to imagine preaching successfully without at least some knowledge of our culture, defined in this particular way.

In former times this web of story and image came in part from classical culture. If in those times one were, for example, to say, "They're like Damon and Pythias," a reasonably well-educated person would know that you were speaking of two close friends. This is no longer the case. I tried the names "Damon and Pythias" out on some very bright young people with no response whatever. Even more widely known in former times were the stories of the Bible. Phrases like "a good Samaritan" or "a Judas kiss" conveyed meaning immediately. One wonders how widely this is still the case. With the same young people I tried "David and Jonathan." One teen said, "Do you mean King David?" but could not remember any Jonathan in the story of David. I then tried *Thelma and Louise* and *Butch Cassidy and the Sundance Kid*. These met with immediate recognition—the teens knew the stories of these films very well, even though the latter film had been made before they were born.[4] If one wants to create in the minds of listeners a picture of friendship, one ought not to refer to Damon and Pythias or David and Jonathan; one ought to mention the movies or, even better, the TV show *Friends*. But one cannot do this without knowledge of mass culture.

Make no mistake; it takes time to become familiar with our culture, even mass culture, and most of us are desperately short of time. Amid the press of ministerial duties, the mountains of ecclesiastical administrivia, and the throng of personal demands, how can anyone blame a minister for not knowing, for example, what "bites" means to a Toronto teenager? It remains true, however, that a preacher who intends to make use of the power of analogy must know the culture in which our people live. An analogy may "fit" the biblical text, but if it does not likewise fit the lives of the hearers it is merely a piece of clever uselessness. The fact that it is difficult or even impossible to know our culture thoroughly is no excuse. Is there any ministerial task that is not difficult if not impossible?

So how do we begin to know our culture? There is an old saying attributed to unnamed rabbis, that the Lord gave us two ears and only one mouth as a sign that we should listen twice as much as we speak. The Lord also gave us two eyes and the same principle applies to them! As they used to tell us at the railroad crossings "Stop, look, and listen!" Imagine, for example, that you are standing in line at the checkout counter of the local supermarket. This is a chronicle of wasted time for most of us, but it can be a surprisingly fruitful opportunity for a little cultural investigation if we open our eyes and ears. What are the people ahead of you in line at the grocery store talking about? Why do you think those topics interest those people? What are the headlines in the supermarket tabloids? They're not all about Elvis sightings and alien abductions. Who are the names in the unlikely headlines, and why would anybody be interested in them? But don't neglect to ask yourself, in passing, why so many in our society believe that Elvis is alive, perhaps more vigorously than many Christians believe Jesus is alive. And why do so many people, on startlingly little evidence, believe in alien beings of massively superior intelligence? Are they seeking, in an increasingly secular society, for the equivalent of angels or demons? Are they perhaps acknowledging a need deeply lodged in the human heart for a savior beyond ourselves? These are spiritual questions! There will also be more serious magazines on the stand. Who is on the cover of *Time* or *Newsweek*? Why are these people there? What have they done to deserve their notoriety or fame? Could God be doing anything through them? Then take a look at the shopping cart behind you. What are people actually buying? What can you deduce about their families and their habits from their purchases? What are likely to be their actual preoccupations, as far as you can tell? Don't take it too seriously; you are not Sherlock Holmes. But Holmes's complaint against Dr. Watson could equally be leveled against most of us: "You see but you do not observe!" If we become observers of our society, rather than merely onlookers, we will, perhaps, with God's mercy, be more fit to preach to it.

By the way, simply observing the contemporary scene is also the best way to get what are usually called "illustrations." Illustrations cribbed from somebody's published collection simply do not fit very well in most of our sermons. What I am speaking about here is the wonderful side benefit of an observer's attitude to the world. If we open our eyes and our ears, the stories, the genuine and believable human stories, will come to us.

Of course, when you are looking at that magazine rack it would not hurt to buy one. I don't really mean the tabloids; from my admittedly limited knowledge of these rags I would say that the headlines are their most interesting feature. (Though even here there is something of value. The contrast between what is on offer in the headlines and what is actually there in the articles is a striking picture of the false promises offered by our society.) But do pick up the *Time* or *Newsweek,* or *Macleans* if you're in Canada, or *Atlantic Monthly* or *Harper's* or . . . Read not only the news sections but the movie reviews and the reports on the arts. Read your daily newspaper as well; Barth was quite right about its usefulness for homiletics. Watch the occasional hit TV show and, oh yes, take out the people who are significant to you to a movie or play or concert. That will be good for more than your sermons! Perhaps the best advice is to talk to—no, make that *listen* to—a teenager. Many teens float in pop culture like a jellyfish; they are positively bathed by it. We hope that they are at the same time developing the vertebrae and muscles to swim against some of the currents, but why not take advantage of their present immersion?

The point of all this is that we as preachers presently exist within our culture. We do not have to *do* anything special or different to gain some knowledge of it. We merely have to open our eyes and ears in order to take advantage of the opportunities of knowing our culture that are almost inescapably there.

Let the accent rest for a minute on the word "almost" in the previous sentence. It is, in fact, possible to escape from the wider culture if we so choose. The trouble is that the clergy are among those who may most easily be tempted to perform the Houdini-like task of escaping from our culture. We achieve this by escaping *from* our culture *into* a particular subculture. The organization in which we work, church or denomination or hospital or whatever, is the particular haven. The fellowship of the like-minded with whom we socialize is very likely to be an extension of that subculture. We cannot avoid nor ought we to bemoan this immersion in a particular subculture. Of course we become passionately involved with our job and our friends; there is nothing wrong with that! It is certainly not my intention to add to the load of guilt that already presses down on so many ministers and priests. But while immersion in all this is inescapable, some of us clergy never come up for air. We know little beyond the front door of the church, and because we know so little of what goes on beyond the front door; we often fail to recognize what exists inside that door. Such people are, almost by definition, limited preachers. Analogical preachers must stick their noses out the church door for at least the occasional breath of fresh, nonecclesiastical air.

KNOW THE SITUATION

While it would be a sad thing unthinkingly to be trapped within a particular Christian subculture, it is important to recognize that it is most frequently within the context of that particular subculture that you will preach. Know well the place that might, if you are not careful, become your prison! It is vital to perform an exegesis of your preaching situation. The most likely such context is a congregation of some sort, but many other settings are possible. I have students who preach regularly in a prison or a chronic care ward for Alzheimer's patients, in a local jail, or to a second-generation service of an immigrant church where all the English speakers are under the age of thirty. You will understand immediately that any of these settings demands a sermon quite different from the one expected in, say, an aging upper-middle-class suburban congregation.

Here is an instrument I give my students to begin to get at the dynamics of their situation:

EXEGESIS OF THE SITUATION

1. Name of institution

2. Type of institution

3. Social and economic makeup of the audience/congregation

4. Social and economic makeup of the surrounding community

5. Age of listeners (rough numbers and % of whole)

   1–12 _____ 13–19 _____ 20–29 _____

   30–39 _____ 40–60 _____ 60+ _____

6. Gender (%) Female _____ Male _____

7. Educational background (highest level attained, % of whole)

   Primary school _____ High school _____

   Postsecondary _____ Postgraduate _____

8. In what people or structures does the power lie in this situation?

9. What are the special ideological/theological, or other emphases, if any, of this institution? (Examples: liberal, conservative, evangelical, the liturgy, missions, social justice, fellowship, the music program)

10. What issues or circumstances are temporarily of special concern to the people of this institution? (Examples: death of teens in a car accident, a proposal to build an addition)

11. What special factors of institutional history might affect the congregation's ability to hear you?

12. Describe the worship style of this congregation or other setting.

13. What expectations of the minister do the people bring with them?

14. What expectations do people have with respect to the sermon?

15. What will the people have difficulty hearing from you?

16. What have the people learned well?

17. What do the people need to learn?

18. In their free time the people of this institution

    like to watch:

    like to read:

    like to listen to:

19. This congregation understands the Bible to be:

20. What hopes or expectations does this group have for the future?

It is not always easy to get this information. But over a period of several years in the same setting, the information will begin to come to us if our eyes and ears are open. Of course, by that time, in our mobile, even rootless culture the information may be outdated. So, like the painters of the Golden Gate Bridge, we start over again.

What do we do with the information? Perhaps the single most useful thing about an exegesis of the situation is that it allows us to love intelligently the people to whom we minister. Hatred can be the fuel of eloquence. There has, perhaps, been no more powerful public speaker in our century than Adolf Hitler. Hitler's eloquence was most certainly based on hatred. There has been, moreover, to our shame and sorrow as a church, no shortage of preachers whose appeal has likewise been based on their ability to inspire hatred for others. But preaching, proper Christian preaching, springs from love. C. S. Lewis wrote a book entitled *The Four Loves*, in this case the four Greek words that might reasonably be translated as "love." Lewis was not writing for preachers; the four loves we must know are different from his, but our preaching too grows from four loves. These are love of God, love of the church, love of words, and love of people. The exegesis of the situation can, if used rightly, lead to a fuller and more intelligent love of the people committed by God and the church to our care.

KNOW YOURSELF

The great American preacher of the last century, Phillips Brooks, once called preaching "truth through personality." This is not a definition with which I resonate. It smacks too much of the elevated pulpit, the lowered lights, and the honeyed baritone pronouncing religious vacuities. But we ought not to imagine that the temptation to push ourselves forward in our preaching is limited only to the highly paid occupants of "first steeple" pulpits. I once had a consultation with a minister in a middle-sized congregation in a small town in Ontario. He told me that he began every sermon with a joke. I asked him why he did this. "So that they will like me" was his plaintive reply. This preacher was only more honest than most of us. How many of our efforts in the pulpit are really designed not to help people love Jesus or rather to know that they are loved by Jesus, but to make them "like" us?

We need a dose of the homiletics of the apostle Paul. Paul knew that people said of him that "his bodily presence is weak, and his speech contemptible" (2 Cor. 10:10). It was not that he despised rhetoric; in fact, he knew and used many rhetorical techniques, and he could admire the skills of the great preacher Apollos. But while he knew that he had a treasure in his preaching he also knew that the treasure was held in nothing more exciting than a clay pot. "We do not proclaim ourselves; we proclaim Jesus Christ as Lord" (2 Cor. 4:5).

A good dose of humility is a homiletical necessity. The trouble is, of course, that it requires more than a little ego strength to stand up in front of a group of people and speak about anything at all, let alone a gospel that will often contradict the wisdom of this world. But ego strength and humility are not necessarily mutually exclusive attributes. Go back to Paul for a minute. He could tell Peter to his face that he was wrong. He had the chutzpah to say of those pressing the Galatians to submit to circumcision, "Why don't these agitators . . . go all the way and castrate themselves!" (Gal. 5:12).[5] He could cheerfully boast of his own ethnic descent and personal piety (Phil. 3:5–6), and of his many sufferings and accomplishments as an ambassador of the gospel (2 Cor. 11: 22–28). But even while engaged in what he himself recognized as boasting, he could confess, "I am speaking as a fool" (2 Cor. 11:21). He knew that his task was to point beyond himself to Christ. It may well be that it was not only the church in Corinth that needed the reminder that the true subject of Christian preaching is not the preacher, but Christ crucified; it may also have been Paul himself. Good preachers, and Paul was a good preacher, preach to themselves before they preach to the congregation.

Thomas Long, in his book *The Witness of Preaching,* identifies as the controlling image for preaching of the sort Karl Barth preferred the word "herald."[6] It is a good biblical image. The Greek verb most commonly translated as preaching, *kerusso,* means quite literally acting as a herald. That which is preached is the herald's message, the *kerygma.* The herald's job is not to present his or her own personality but rather to proclaim in as faithful a manner as possible the word that is sent. The personality of the preacher is not a matter of any great importance in this view. What matters to the herald is faithfulness to the gospel message, which alone has the power to save. Any attempt to impress the congregation with the preacher's personality is actually counterproductive. In this model of preaching one would have to modify Brooks's dictum to "truth in spite of personality."

There may be a practical as well as a theological objection to preaching that accords too high a role to the preacher's personality. David Buttrick in his massive work *Homiletic* even directs the preacher to avoid personal illustrations in preaching. To tell of one's own experiences is to introduce the very real possibility of misplaced consciousness in the listeners.[7] The congregation's attention is torn away from whatever point the preacher is trying to communicate to the preacher's self.

There are other controlling images for the preacher besides "herald." Long also identifies the "therapist" and the "storyteller" as possibilities.

His favored image, as one might guess from the title of his book, is that of "witness." In all these models the personality of the preacher is of greater importance than for the "herald."[8] But every word is somehow an incarnate one. Even the personality of a herald does have some bearing on the way a message is received. We do indeed, as the apostle Paul says, have the treasure of the gospel in clay pots, but it still pays to consider what kind of clay we have and are.

For the purposes of this book the most important influence of the preacher's self on preaching may be this: the kind of persons we are affects materially the analogies we are prepared to see in the text. I as a middle-class white, male, relatively conservative Reformed minister will catch sight of certain potential analogies. A vigorous feminist, a third-world liberation theologian, a conservative Roman Catholic will see others.[9] We do not approach scripture naked; we are clothed in our personality, our preconceptions, and our presuppositions. It is impossible to do otherwise.[10] Many scholars speak of a "hermeneutical circle," or perhaps better, a "hermeneutical spiral," since the purpose of interpretation is not, after all, to go around endlessly in the same circle. We take to the biblical text our presuppositions and read the text in light of those presuppositions. We then attempt to examine ourselves in light of what we have read in order to test the adequacy of those presuppositions. The presuppositions will in all probability be materially altered. We then go back to the text with those altered presuppositions, and so on. Under the guidance of the Holy Spirit the result of this process is growth. But this process is difficult or even impossible if we do not examine ourselves. John Calvin compares the Bible to a mirror—what use is a mirror if we do not examine ourselves in it? The preacher who intends to preach analogically had better be prepared to perform three exegeses: the text, the situation, and the self.

It is possible that of the three forms of exegesis, the exegesis of the self is the most difficult. We quote Robbie Burns: "Oh wad some power the giftie gie us / to see oursels as others see us!" but often we would rather return the gift unopened! We humans do have a capacity, highly developed in some cases, to ignore the obvious about ourselves. You will see below the instrument that I use to help students to engage in an exegesis of the self. As you will see, there is in the instrument a question that asks what issues we might be tempted to overemphasize. I have had several students who were completely swallowed up by particular issues; their preoccupations, shall we say, made themselves known to new acquaintances immediately after the words "How do you do?" if not before. None of them identified their manias in answer to that question. While it is fair to say that more balanced people do a better job of examining themselves, it remains true that most of us need the help of others, trusted others, to see ourselves at all clearly. Study of the Bible is best done with others as a corrective to our fancies, study of ourselves is likewise best done with others as a corrective to our blindness.

You may not wish actually to carry out the exegesis of the self at this point. If you do, however, there are just a few points about the instrument that should be mentioned. The instrument asks you to "label" yourself in certain ways. It is true that to a degree all labels are lies. They never adequately represent a whole person, and many of us feel rightly uncomfortable with them. It is also true that labels vary wildly according to the standards of the person doing the labeling. I once lost a church member who told me he couldn't stand my "persistent liberalism." Shortly thereafter I was called the most conservative man in the denomination in a committee of the national church. It's amazing how far right I had moved in a few months! Most people who are not rigid and predictable party-liners have had similar experiences. Moreover, the answer to the whole question is affected by noting which of the several contexts in which we live we are speaking about. For example, I am more conservative relative to the college in which I teach than in relation to the denomination to which I belong. Our place on an ideological or theological spectrum depends in large part on which spectrum we are speaking about.

I believe, however, that it is useful to try to locate our position on the spectrum of opinion within our particular contexts. It is even more useful to compare ourselves with the way others see us. Questions concerning this contrast, as you will notice, form part of the instrument.

For the preacher, of course, the most significant context will be the one in which she or he preaches. For the purpose of this exercise, the setting with which you are asked to compare yourself is the setting for which you did the "Exegesis of the Situation."

EXEGESIS OF THE SELF

1. Name _____

2. Age _____

3. Gender _____

4. Socioeconomic background

5. Key family relationships and their nature

6. I read (types of periodicals, books)

7. My congregation reads (types of periodicals, books)

8. I listen to (type or types of music)

9. My congregation listens to (type or types of music)

10. I watch (types of TV shows, movies)

11. My congregation watches (types of TV shows, movies)

12. I relate most easily to people who are: ages _____

    gender _____ family circumstances _____

    education _____ other _____

13. I have most difficulty relating to ages _____ gender _____

    family circumstances _____

    education _____ other _____

14. I would label myself as _____ ,

    _____ (examples: liberal, conservative, evangelical, feminist, or other categories)

15 Others would tend to see me as _____ ,

    _____ (examples: liberal, conservative, evangelical, feminist, or other categories)

16. What issues or pastoral situations might I be tempted to avoid?

17. What issues or pastoral situations might I be tempted to overemphasize?

18. My personality will be a help to me in my ministry in the following ways:

19. My personality will be a hindrance to me in my ministry in the following ways:

20. If there is a perceived conflict between the Bible and the world-view of my society or between the Bible and the opinions of my particular subgroup in society, I would tend to say:

    The Bible is wrong _____

    My society is wrong _____

    Other _____

21. I understand the Bible to be:

22. My congregation understands the Bible to be:

23. What common ground exists between my congregation and me?

three

The Other Side
of the Analogy

KNOW THE TEXT

An exegesis performed as the foundation of a sermon to some congregation of God's people will be subtly but substantially different from an exegesis prepared for a course in Bible. The aim will not be a cool, dispassionate, objective exposition of the literary or historical significance of the text, as if such an exegesis were possible. The aim is the encounter with the living God in which the minister is addressed by God and through which experience the congregation too might find itself likewise addressed. Such an exegesis will make the fullest possible use of the preacher's intellectual and academic resources, but in the end it will be primarily a spiritual exercise.

The book for our time on the spirituality of the preacher is yet to be written. While I know that I am not the person to write that book, I can make several guesses about what the book will contain. I believe that it will locate that spirituality at the conjunction of the three exegeses outlined here. The spirituality of the devout preacher lives where the text, the situation, and the self come together. I further believe that the book will urge on its readers a careful discipline of prayer and meditation. When, as a relatively young man, I was appointed to my present chair I received, as one might expect, a good deal of advice from grizzled veterans of the church. I truly valued it. But the best advice I received was a succinct statement from a minister even younger and less experienced than I: "Stephen, tell them they can't preach if they don't pray." In the long run nothing could be more true than this advice. The preacher's prayer life will grow out of the text, the situation, and the self.

It has often been argued, by Dietrich Bonhoeffer, for example, that the preacher must study and meditate on the scriptures other than the preaching texts for the week.[1] It is dangerous to the spirit to read the Bible only as a means to an end, in this case the preparation of the weekly homily or sermon. A spiritually mature minister or priest does not read the Bible only as a prelude to practical homiletics. I am not yet such a person, but I do know already that to read the Bible only to get material for next Sunday's sermon is damaging to the soul. Preachers who do this dry up.

My late father once told me, "Preach from your overflow!" He had grown up on a farm in dry western Saskatchewan, where it was necessary to pump up pure water by hand from a deep well. (Undrinkable alkaline water was always at hand in the slough; there may be a parable here.) To reach for the waiting buckets at the first slight flow of water was always a mistake. The flow stopped as soon as the overeager farm boy dropped the pump handle. It was necessary, and in the long run easiest, to pump long enough and hard enough to get a good steady stream going so that the basin was full and overflowing. Then and only then could one safely stoop to take away the water for the family's needs.

This is not to suggest, however, that the careful exegesis of a text or texts in preparation for preaching is unspiritual. A careful and thorough exegesis of the texts for the weekly sermon forms part of a healthy spiritual diet. There is also nothing more practical for the preacher than a thorough study of the biblical text. A constant complaint of weak preachers is "What am I going to preach on next Sunday?" The complaint of their parishioners is different; they know what the pastor will preach on—some variation of "the same old thing every Sunday." The preacher who studies the scripture regularly and faithfully does not have the first complaint, and it is far less likely that the parishioners will have the second. Preachers who get in the habit of good exegesis will indeed have a problem. They will have so much homiletical material that it will be difficult to know what to leave out!

But this too is a good thing. Experienced clergy know all too well that there inevitably comes a week or a month when too many things just seem to happen at once. There is a serious illness in the congregation, as well as several deaths, a nasty fight on the governing board, two denominational committees, a service club luncheon, and next Sunday is Christmas or Easter. You get the picture. Moreover, there will be times when, despite all our spiritual disciplines, we do dry up spiritually until we begin to resemble Ezekiel's valley of the bones—"And they were very dry." But Sunday's coming—it rolls around with a fair degree of predictability immediately after Saturday, and no extensions are allowed on *this* assignment. This is not to deny that there are times when the pressures of ministry are simply so great that the wisest course of action is to take time off for spiritual, psychological, and physical recreation. The alternative may be to blow out or burn out, and this helps no one. But apart from these major crises, we do for the most part carry on through those weeks and months. What do we do when that week or that month comes? And rest assured, it will come. If we have been faithful in our exegesis, we will have an overflow to draw on, and the congregation need not go thirsty. It isn't that different from the advice Joseph gave Pharaoh during the seven years of plenty. It isn't that different from saving money for the proverbial rainy day.

Late in his life Sir Isaac Newton was asked how he had conceived the law of universal gravitation. He replied, "By thinking on it continually." The process of thinking in an organized and methodical manner on a text is exegesis. There is no substitute in preaching for thinking on a text—if not continually, at least for some length of time in an organized and methodical manner.

What follows is an exegetical method that you might wish to use in your weekly study. Many books on preaching suggest an exegetical method,[2] and all clergy are taught some form of exegetical method in their seminary or Bible college days. I do not suggest for a minute that the method I suggest here is the only or even the best method. I do suggest, though, that it is necessary that you adopt some carefully thought out method and adhere to it. It is not that it is impossible to preach a good sermon without sound exegesis. It is, however, hard to imagine preaching a good sermon *regularly* without such a discipline.

There was a young man, who was taken out to play tennis for the first time by an expert player. At one point, the rookie rushed the net and the expert coolly dropped a lob over his head. The rookie turned, dashed back on the court, and without looking swiped wildly at the ball and sent it screaming, Wimbledon style, into the far corner of his opponent's court. Point! But because he had never learned the proper mechanics of a swing there was no way that he could repeat the shot or even succeed with much easier shots on a regular basis. When the expert tried to teach the young man the discipline of a proper swing, the novice found that he actually hit the ball less well than if he swung naturally and wildly. He knew well enough that if he persevered he would eventually gain the proper form and improve as a player, but he balked at the tedium of learning a new swing. The no-longer-young man still can't play tennis, but he knows that it's his (my!) fault. It is one thing not to want to undergo the discipline of learning a sport. It is quite another for a minister or priest to refuse the discipline of biblical study. There is no way to be an effective preacher without discipline and hard work.

It is undeniably true that the hypothetical average preacher does not have much time to devote to the weekly exegesis for a sermon. Deane

Kemper is probably pushing the upper limits for most busy pastors when he states, "It is important that the pastor learn to do respectable and responsible exegesis for a sermon in four to five hours' time."[3] Some clergy may be picturing their calendars and thinking, Four or five hours! Where can I find four or five hours? Without attempting to defend Kemper's exact figures, it is certainly true that the minister who is serious about the business of preaching will find the time to put significant hours into biblical study. The truth is, we find time for what matters to us.

We clergy often let our calendars get positively bloated. There is a particular temptation for the pastor to be *seen* to be busy. There are psychic rewards for the pastor who is always out and about and "with the people." We earn the praise of many of our people in this way. "Our former minister wore out two cars when he was at our church!" What makes the temptation so insidiously effective is that the temptation to sheer busyness so often involves what is manifestly good and indeed our pastoral duty. There is always something—no, many somethings—that we genuinely ought to be doing. But is any one of these things as important as listening for the word of God? Is there anything more truly significant than reading and praying and writing so that on Sunday a congregation of God's people will hear not just our voice but, by a miracle of the Holy Spirit, God's voice?

When we are forced to choose the truly vital over the seemingly significant we do somehow find time for what matters to us. When I was in the pastorate I allowed myself to get too busy with the general pastoralia of a growing congregation. I simply had to be present at every church committee and activity, or so I thought. At the time, my two sons were three and one years of age. One day the three-year-old came into the room where I was sitting. He picked up a book and said, "I'm Daddy. This is my Bible."

How cute; he's imitating me, I thought.

"I'm going to a meeting," he said. Very realistic, but not nearly as cute!

Then he put the book down, looked me in the eyes, and said with gentle sadness, "But maybe tomorrow I'll stay home with my boys."

It felt as if I had been stabbed.

Bless me, for I have sinned as a father. Mea culpa, mea maxima culpa.

I got up, found my calendar, and began drawing lines through many of the engagements. The church did just fine without my presence at all those activities. The moral of this story is not simply that we must pay attention to those whom we love or we risk losing them, though that is a lesson well worth learning. It is that we can, if we truly want, cut down our busyness for the sake of what matters to us.

We can hear the voice of God when we study the Bible faithfully and diligently. Listening for that voice matters as very little else matters. It is the echo of that voice that should whisper through all our ministerial activities. There is nothing more important than listening for that voice. If we believe that God's voice matters that much we will indeed find time to listen for it. We sometimes ask, "How can I afford the time to do a thorough exegesis of the text?" The real question is, How can I afford not to?

For most of us, when life actually works there is surprisingly often at the bottom of that success a good habit. When we fall into or rather climb into good habits, from personal hygiene to spiritual development, life simply functions better. The activity that becomes a good habit may look rather daunting at first. The child says, "But do I have to brush after *every* meal?" But when brushing becomes a habit, it is easy, even second nature, and the teeth are healthier. The student or new minister who contemplates a method of exegesis may say, "But do I have to do all that before every sermon?" I do not assert that study becomes second nature or even easy if it becomes a habit; I do affirm that it becomes manageable. And the sermons are much better! It is vital for the student or new minister to develop good habits from the beginning, for we all know that it is far easier to learn good habits than to break bad ones. One of the best habits is the one Thomas Long calls "the exegetical habit."[4]

In my denomination ministers who are having grave difficulties in their congregations are usually sent for psychological counseling. Such counseling is genuinely useful. However, clergy troubles frequently stem not from psychological instability, but from a variety of other factors. Some troubled ministers suffer from sheer laziness or lack of interpersonal skills. A surprising number of priests and ministers are simply rude to their parishioners! Many of the most useful ministerial skills ought to have been learned in kindergarten. An appreciable number of clergy, however, particularly in traditions that, like my own, emphasize the pulpit ministry, get into trouble because they are, to put it bluntly, lousy preachers. It has been my responsibility, as a member of church visitation committees, to listen to the complaints of far too many dissatisfied members of far too many churches. From them I hear again and again some variation on "We're not being fed." These people feel in their heart of hearts that they are not getting the kind of preaching that they believe the church and their families deserve.

The judicatories or church authorities, in addition to requiring psychological counseling, sometimes refer their ministers to continuing education events in homiletics. Even more clergy are wise enough voluntarily to attend such events before there is trouble in their churches. I do not deny the usefulness of continuing education events in homiletics (even the ones I lead!). But the participants at these events all too often focus on technique, as if a narrative style or an inductive structure, or better "moves" could cure our homiletical woes. Of course, I do not deny that preachers ought to pay attention to such matters. Moreover, the fault in this concentration is not entirely with the participants; we professors of homiletics who lead these sessions delight in such matters. Some clergy, and this cannot be blamed on the leaders, even show up at homiletics workshops with only one burning question: "Heard any good illustrations lately?" But if people are not being fed by the sermons they hear, the problem is probably not at heart a matter of style, structure, or technique, and still less of winning little anecdotes. Sawdust is not rendered nutritious by artful presentation! It is very likely that the minister or priest in trouble because of poor preaching has had little or nothing intelligent or spiritually edifying to say. There is no cure for this ill but disciplined study, particularly of the Bible. Technique deserves our attention, but there is no salvation in technique. The best advice I can give a minister who is becoming aware of homiletical weakness is, "Double the time you spend in your study and spend most of that time working on the biblical text." It is the most time- and energy-effective investment a preacher can make. We dare not forget that the ministry is a spiritual office. In carrying out a spiritual commitment, the truly spiritual is the most practical thing one can do. There is nothing more truly practical than the spiritual commitment of biblical study.

The fact remains that it is difficult to find time for thorough sermon preparation in general and for exegesis in particular. There are ways to make our limited time budget stretch farther, however. First, there is the question of choice of texts for sermons. Some preachers select texts almost randomly. On Monday or Tuesday, or even later in a given week, the preacher finally settles on a text for Sunday's sermon and begins work on the text. Call this person the occasional preacher. At first sight this method has the advantage of enabling the minister to respond to the needs or circumstances or interests that emerge in that particular week. Relevance is the hoped-for result. It doesn't always work that way, unfortunately. For one thing, such a strategy, if the word "strategy" even applies to this hit-and-miss procedure, is by definition reactive rather than proactive. Effective leadership, by contrast, even pulpit leadership, is usually proactive rather than reactive. Moreover, in practice the minister who preaches only occasional sermons usually struggles and struggles and hits on whatever text seems best that particular week. "Whatever seems best" may more and more become whatever coincides with the minister's preoccupations and prejudices. The specter of the well-ridden hobbyhorse looms on the homiletical horizon. That expert tempter, the old devil Screwtape, recognized the type at its worst:

> The Vicar is a man who has been so long engaged in watering down the faith to make it easier for a supposedly incredulous and hard-headed congregation that it is now he who shocks his parishioners with his unbelief, not vice-versa. He has undermined many a soul's Christianity. His conduct of the services is also admirable. In order to spare the laity all "difficulties" he has deserted both the lectionary and the appointed psalms and now, without noticing it, revolves endlessly round the little treadmill of his fifteen favourite psalms and twenty favourite lessons. We are thus safe from the danger that any truth not already familiar to him and to his flock should ever reach them through Scripture.[5]

That is the spiritual problem that may, though not necessarily will, afflict the occasional preacher. But once again the spiritual has practical consequences. To start from scratch each week wastes an enormous amount of time and energy. Imagine that you spend one hour a week trying to decide what text to preach from. Assume that holidays and weeks in which you have to preach more than once balance each other out. That means that you have expended fifty-two valuable hours before you have even begun to study the texts themselves. In fact, the estimate of fifty-two hours is far too conservative. Double that time is far more likely to be accurate. What minister could not profitably use one hundred plus working hours in a typical year?

The answer to both the spiritual and the practical problem are indirectly suggested by Screwtape: Use a lectionary! But before dealing with the advantages of the lectionary, let me put in a good word for two ancient homiletical patterns, the sermon series, especially the doctrinal series, and the *lectio continua*. I mention these patterns here because adopting them will indeed save the modern preacher time. There are, of course, more pressing and serious reasons for choosing them than merely the saving of time and energy, however.

Preaching a series of doctrinal sermons is an ancient and honorable pattern in the Christian church; in the early church it appeared most frequently in the form of catechetical instruction to candidates for baptism. To give but one example, in the period before Easter Saint Ambrose of Milan preached each year a series of daily catechetical sermons to candidates for baptism. These sermons included instruction on the Lord's Prayer and the Apostles' Creed. To the newly baptized he then preached a series of six sermons on the sacraments. One presumes that it was sermon series of this sort that formed the preparation for baptism of Ambrose's most famous convert, Saint Augustine. Other catechetical sermons that survive to this day were preached by Saint Cyril of Jerusalem, Saint John Chrysostom, and the great biblical scholar, Theodore of Mopsuestia.[6] The Reformers also preached series of catechetical sermons, and the practice carries on to the present day. A fine example of the modern doctrinal series is the exposition of the Apostles' Creed by the great German theologian and preacher Helmut Thielicke, *I Believe: The Christian's Creed*.[7]

Sermon series need not be based on the creed, however. I have heard preachers organize series around the emotions, pressing social issues, ethical difficulties, and even the stained-glass windows in the church sanctuary. Whatever the form, preaching a series can save time because one organizes the series as a whole at the beginning of the process and loses no further time in searching for Sunday texts. More significantly, it allows our investment in time and study to work more efficiently. The reading that we do for one week may very well throw light on and be useful for several sermons later in the series. It is the homiletical version of compound interest. Particularly with respect to doctrinal series, the study of the biblical text can be richly supplemented by the reading of works of systematic theology. I know a minister who recently undertook the discipline of preaching through the Apostles' Creed. The series allowed him the time and motivated him to invest the time in working through several extensive works on Christian doctrine that he would never have mastered without the stimulus of sermon preparation. He probably understood them better as a result of having to make practical use of these works Sunday by Sunday than if he had merely read them as part of a seminary course in theology. He was, he affirms, greatly enriched by the experience.

More important, congregations are enriched by such preaching. It is true that contemporary homiletics tends to be more concerned with creating an experience than with persuading the congregation to accept an argument. Preachers want the congregation to experience the presence of God rather than to accept a series of propositions about God. But good preaching can—in fact, preaching *should*—appeal to both heart and head.

I believe we preachers tend to overestimate the biblical and theological knowledge of the people in our congregations but to underestimate their intelligence and interest. While the extent of the thirst for ordered knowledge and some sort of coherent theology varies from person to person in the congregation, it is pretty widely present and it is not, I believe, being satisfied in much of our preaching. I believe that there is a desire for *di-*

dache, instruction in the Christian faith.[8] This may be met by the concentrated doctrinal preaching that is provided by a series.

The second possibility, lectio continua, means, quite simply, reading and preaching through a book in its canonical order. It was the preferred homiletical strategy of many leaders of the Reformation, particularly in the Reformed or Calvinist tradition. In a city that had accepted the reformation, particularly of the Reformed variety, the lectionary was abandoned in favor of lectio continua reading and preaching. The lectionary might well be retained in a Lutheran city, but there too lectio continua was practiced. Luther himself, as a liturgical conservative by nature, retained the lectionary and preached in an expository fashion on its texts, but he also preached lectio continua through several books of the Bible. This would remain a classic form of Protestant preaching for several centuries.

Lectio continua was not, however, an invention of the Protestant Reformation. Many of the fathers of the church engaged in this practice. So the greatest preacher of the ancient church, John Chrysostom (Golden Mouth) of Antioch and Constantinople, was renowned for his expository sermons on biblical texts. Chrysostom preached ninety sermons on the Gospel of John, eighty-nine on Matthew, forty-four on the Acts of the Apostles, sixty-seven on Genesis, and so on. The greatest theologian of Western Christianity, Augustine of Hippo, was likewise a preacher of great fame. While he preached on particular texts selected for the occasion during the festivals of the newly developing church year, Augustine normally preached according to the pattern of lectio continua. We still possess, for example, one hundred and twenty-four of his sermons on the Gospel of John.

It may be that in preaching lectio continua Chrysostom, Augustine, and many other preachers of the early church were following a pattern that Christianity inherited from Judaism. The synagogue was at heart a house established for the public reading and explanation of scripture.

> The reading of a portion of the torah on every Sabbath and festival seems to have been a regular feature of the synagogue from the outset, and may have constituted *the* fundamental reason for the emergence of that institution.[9]

It is probable that a pattern of reading through the five books of the Pentateuch in order was established in many synagogues well before the Christian era, though scholars are no longer confident that one can precisely identify a three-year lectionary cycle.[10] Perhaps the earliest evidence of lectio continua reading and exposition of scripture can be found in Nehemiah 8. There Ezra, together with a number of helpers, read through the

Torah and interpreted it (perhaps only by means of a running translation of the Hebrew into Aramaic) consecutively. Even if one comes to a low estimate of the historicity of the book of Nehemiah, one would surely want to say that this account probably does reflect early liturgical practice.

The present popularity of lectionary-based preaching should not prevent the preacher from considering the potential usefulness of lectio continua. A practice as ancient as this deserves some respect for its venerable age if nothing else. It is true that in the wrong hands the pattern can be stultifyingly tedious and a too-detailed treatment of the text can grind a text into mush. The puritan divine Charles Manton preached *one hundred ninety sermons on Psalm 119 alone!*[11] I do not for a minute advocate the preaching of such detailed series. Nevertheless, there are certain real advantages to preaching lectio continua. The main advantage is that the scriptural texts under consideration are treated in their canonical contexts. As we shall see, context is one of the prime determinants of meaning. A colleague at Knox College used to say, "Position is hermeneutic."[12] That is to say that the position of text relative to the texts that surround it is the clue to its meaning. In the lectionary the context, that is to say, the texts that surround a particular passage, is determined not by the canon but by the lectionary itself. Shifting the context of a particular passage by reading it together with the other lectionary texts may therefore also substantially shift its perceived meaning.

Consider the story of creation and fall in Genesis 2 and 3, for example. We have in those two chapters in their canonical context and order one coherent story. We almost invariably ignore the flow of the story as a whole in worship, however. We deal with it in discrete bits that appear in the company, not of what the "author" or "redactor" of Genesis intended, but of a variety of texts from the rest of scripture. Here is what the lectionary in use in my church does with (to) these texts:

> Genesis 2:15–17; 3:1–7 are read on the First Sunday in Lent
> in Year A.
> Genesis 2:18–24 appears on Proper 22 of Year B.
> Genesis 3:8–15 appears on Proper 5 of Year B.

How can anyone get a sense of the narrative as a whole from such a disjointed reading of the story? But then the purpose of the lectionary is not to give a reader a sense of the canonical text of the Old Testament reading in particular. Since the canonical context is pretty effectually stripped away, the accompanying texts of the lectionary are left to supply the contextual clues to the meaning of the passage. Consider the texts that appear with the Genesis readings on Lent 1: Psalm 32; Romans 5:12–19; and Matthew 4:1–11. In the book of Genesis, the story is set in the context of the creation of a cosmos in which all things are repeatedly called good, and in which the Lord delights to shower blessings on Adam and Eve. The lectionary texts are a penitential psalm, Paul's theological exposition of the entry of sin into the world through one man, Adam, and the story of the temptation of Jesus. In the lectionary, the story's vital connection to a good creation is lost and the fragment of the Genesis story gains a much darker and more somber tone. There is certainly no "creation spirituality" here! Moreover, the exegetically dubious identification of serpent and Satan is pretty well unavoidable given the juxtaposition of these texts.[13]

The point here is not that the framers of the lectionary "messed up" with respect to Genesis 2 and 3 (though that is certainly a possible conclusion). It is that by supplying a context different from that provided by the canon itself the lectionary inevitably alters the listener's perception of the meaning of the text. A lectionary by its very nature can do no other; it is the nature of a lectionary to supply a series of texts that relate primarily to the day and season of the church year. The degree to which the alteration in meaning caused by the lectionary is significant will vary from Sunday to Sunday and from text to text. In the case of Lent 1 in Year A, the Gospel and Epistle readings do not suffer as serious a shift in meaning as does the reading from Genesis. The temptation and fall of Adam are, it could be argued, the appropriate context of those passages within the canon as a whole. This result would be fairly typical. The lectionary follows the church year, which is for the most part a running narrative of the life and ministry of Jesus Christ. The organizing principle is primarily Christocentric. The lectionary therefore concentrates on the Gospel texts and at many key points uses the Old Testament texts in a complementary fashion. This strategy means that, relatively speaking, the New Testament texts suffer less and the Old Testament texts suffer more from the kind of distortion of meaning we have been discussing.

Lectio continua is less prone, though not immune, to this kind of contextual distortion. Inappropriate pairing of texts can still affect the perceived meaning of texts preached lectio continua: there is no perfect method of selecting texts. It can, however, help the congregation to grasp the canonical context of the preaching text. Coupled with the interpretative advantage of lectio continua, there is the practical advantage I mentioned earlier—the devotion of time and energy to understanding of a biblical text can be considered as an investment. With lectio continua the investment in understanding a particular book of the Bible can be "amortized" over a greater number of sermons.

There remains the use of the lectionary. Let me declare my bias immediately. I value the lectionary, have preached from it regularly, and am a contributor to a lectionary resource journal.[14] I believe there are huge advantages to following it faithfully. I am, however, dismayed by the attitudes of some lectionary enthusiasts.[15] "The lectionary, the whole lectionary, and nothing but the lectionary!" is their cry. One can preach responsibly, faithfully, and intelligently without ever going near the Common Lectionary or any other lectionary. The history of preaching and the present practice of many faithful preachers make this manifestly clear.

It does seem to me, however, that there are a number of significant advantages to using the lectionary, and it is possible by intelligent study to minimize the disadvantages. An obvious advantage is that there are a huge number of resources available for the preacher who wishes to follow the lectionary. A visit to a church bookstore will quickly show you the extent of these resources: shelf after shelf of books produced by excellent biblical scholars and homileticians. Several journals exist whose primary mission is to aid the preacher in interpreting the lectionary text. These also provide liturgical resources for the busy pastor so that prayers and even hymns and children's stories can be woven together into a coherent whole. Beyond Gutenberg, the Internet and a whole series of local bulletin boards provide forums for the computer literate to discuss the lectionary texts. In fact, so enormous is the range of resources available that it becomes something of a temptation. The minister or priest may depend on these materials rather than on his or her own study. Secondhand study will generally produce but a counterfeit sermon.

Nonetheless, there are other advantages. At least one curriculum enables a church to organize its entire Christian education program around the lectionary, so the proclamation and education of the congregation can be fully integrated. Another advantage is that the lectionary is ecumenical—its use crosses denominational lines. Once again there is a danger lurking behind the advantage. Most of us recognize that the real divisions in the church are not between denominations, but within them. The possibility is that clergy who value things ecumenical are their own "tribe" within the wider church. Getting together with clergy of other traditions to study the lectionary texts may therefore still be a fellowship of the like-minded.

The chief advantage of the lectionary, however, is theological: it exposes preacher and congregation to a broad range of texts that cover most of the main narrative and theological themes of the Bible. The disciplined use of the lectionary will necessarily expose the congregation to texts that the minister or priest might very well be tempted to avoid. It is not the case that the lectionary covers everything in the Bible—what three-year preaching program could? But the sample is reasonably representative of the Bible as a whole. It cannot, in truth, be entirely representative. Those charged with the selection of texts for the lectionary or any other project will inevitably make their choices according to what they have come to believe is most significant about the Bible. But no process of selection is immune from this reality; every selection of material is necessarily also a distortion. What one can say is this: The Christocentric focus of the lectionary has been widely satisfactory within the community of believers. There is no reason to suppose that any other selection would be less arbitrary and more generally acceptable.

One other point should be made at this time: The Common Lectionary incorporates within itself a considerable measure of lectio continua. Each of the three years focuses on one of the Synoptic Gospels, which is read lectio continua for considerable portions of the church year. The same principle is applied from time to time to parts of the Gospel of John, the book of Acts, several of the epistles, and occasionally to the Old Testament lessons. Where this occurs the advantages of lectio continua are also present. The preacher could very appropriately choose to preach on those texts which are treated in this fashion rather than the complementary texts. Though all this is true, the preacher who is anxious that the congregation should gain a more profound understanding of the Old Testament on its own terms will probably have to abandon the lectionary for at least a period of time.

It is also true that while there are significant disadvantages to the lectionary; there are means of counteracting some of the problems with the lectionary and living with the rest. An excellent resource on lectionary preaching is Eugene Lowry's *Living with the Lectionary*.[16] Anyone contemplating preaching on the lectionary should consult that resource.

AN EXEGETICAL METHOD

We proceed now to the exegesis of the text itself. It is organized around a series of ten questions. I have found that on average five or six of these questions are helpful for any given text. Which five or six are useful varies from text to text. It is impossible to know ahead of time which ones will be useful. If a question seems to be getting you nowhere, drop it and proceed to the next one. The typical preacher has very little time to waste! I would suggest, however, that you go through the process first without the aid of commentaries or other resources. Such works have a tendency to channel excessively our creativity. Commentaries are also often written not primarily for the preacher or for the believing community but with the academic guild in mind. After you have answered the questions as best you can, then turn to the secondary resources as a check on your own work.

So down to work!

1. How much am I going to deal with?

Some of the following subquestions may help you determine the limits of the passage:

a. How does the passage differ from what comes before and after it?
b. Is this passage a particular literary form? (See question 3.)
c. Does it have a coherent and complete internal structure? (See question 4.)
d. Is there a change in place between this passage and what surrounds it?
e. Is there a change of characters between this passage and what surrounds it?
f. Is there a change of subject matter between this passage and what surrounds it?
g. Is there a repetition of a key word or phrase (*inclusio*) at the beginning and end of the passage?
h. Is there an indicator of time at the beginning or end of this passage?

Answering question 1 is necessary for purely practical reasons; we have to decide how much of the text we are actually going to read on Sunday morning. Considering it is also the first step toward uncovering the meaning of the passage. Some scholars call this process "cutting" the text, a term we shall adopt for brevity's sake.[17] A passage's meaning and tone can be radically altered by cutting the text in different places. For example, at an ordination in my own denomination, there is about a 50 percent chance that the account of Isaiah's call in chapter 6 will be read aloud. What a magnificent text it is for such an occasion—the vision of the Lord high and lifted up, the smoke drifting from the altar forming in the mind's eye the robes of the divine majesty! The seraphim cry out, "Holy, holy, holy is the LORD of hosts; the whole earth is full of his glory." Isaiah is rightly oppressed by his own and the people's unworthiness, but a seraphim lays a coal from the altar on his unclean lips and his guilt and sin are taken away. The question comes, "Whom shall I send, and who will go for us?" And Isaiah responds, "Here am I; send me!" And here at the end of verse 8, they cut the reading! Fine, stirring stuff this is, very encouraging for the new-fledged reverend.

But the passage continues; God gives Isaiah a particular word:

Go and say to this people:
    "Keep listening, but do not comprehend;
    keep looking but do not understand."
Make the mind of this people dull,
    and stop their ears,
    and shut their eyes,
so that they may not look with their eyes,
    and listen with their ears,
and comprehend with their minds,
    and turn and be healed.

Not a very encouraging message for a new preacher after all! What an enormous difference there is between a text that ends at verse 8 and one that carries on through verse 13! The cutting of the text profoundly affects the meaning of the passage in this and in many other cases. My experience as a listener to sermons suggests that inappropriate cutting of the texts is one of the most common means of misrepresenting the text.

Using the lectionary does not absolve one from the duty and necessity of cutting the text responsibly. One of the weakest characteristics of the Common Lectionary is its peculiar cutting of the lections. Sometimes lections begin or end in the middle of a thought for no perceptible reason. Occasionally the reason for the cut is obvious: the framers don't like nastiness and trouble. So, for example, the psalm for Pentecost is Psalm 104:24–34, 35b. Here is the missing half verse, 35a: "Let sinners be consumed from the earth, and let the wicked be no more."[18] But anyone who has read the psalms as they really are knows that imprecations against the ungodly and the enemy are a regular and troubling feature of this poetry. Can any accurate representation of the psalms or of scripture as a whole systematically ignore such passages?

One might argue that since selection is necessary in any preaching program, it makes sense to select the more obviously edifying portions of scripture for use in the pulpit. But if the scripture functions as a mirror, do we perceive an accurate picture of ourselves in a glass from which the hatred and anger are removed? If the psalms and many other texts are allowed to speak honestly about the human condition as it really is, not merely as we would like it to be, the analogical preacher will be more able likewise to speak honestly of humanity in our own age. In the end, only realism about humanity is either convincing or interesting in the Bible. Honest preachers dare not abandon realism. Censoring the Bible is a terrible mistake.

The problem is far from insuperable, however. Those whose traditions allow some freedom with respect to the lectionary (who live with the lectionary rather than being married to it) are able to alter the boundaries of the text slightly. Those whose traditions demand a more rigorous obedience to its dictates may at least consider the question of where the text ought to be cut and may allow a fuller text than the lectionary selection to shape their sermons.

Cutting the text appropriately is often very easy; in many cases it takes longer to explain how to perform the operation than actually to do it. In other cases it is very difficult to determine where a text should be cut. The various subquestions listed above can be used to help determine the limits of the text. Here are a few practice exercises to develop your skills:

(1) Apply the questions to Isaiah 6. Where would you end the reading?

(2) The lectionary gives as the Gospel reading for Epiphany 7 in Year B Mark 2:1–12. Is this a justifiable division of the text?

(3) You are going to preach from the parable of the dishonest steward, which begins at Luke 16:1. Where will you stop reading?

(4) Cut Luke 12 into pericopes suitable for preaching.

2. How does this passage fit into its literary surroundings?

What is the theological significance of the placement of this passage at this particular point?

This is almost always an interesting and fruitful question. Older forms of biblical criticism virtually ignored the question. Biblical scholars used to speak of "catchword connections" as if these were theologically meaningless. Newer methods such as narrative and rhetorical criticism, on the other hand, consider very carefully the issue of the placement of texts in the scripture. They understand a biblical book to be a carefully crafted whole, within which the arrangement of the parts is highly significant. Position is indeed hermeneutic! So fruitful is this question for preaching that I will deal with it at a later point at some length.

For now, consider the placement of the little story of the widow's mite, Mark 12:41–44, a favorite text for stewardship sermons. By itself it is an example story; it holds up, apparently for our imitation, the account of a widow who gives all she has into the Temple treasury. The woman's action is admirable. We modern preachers generally point to her and say, "Go and do thou likewise!"

It looks a little different when you consider the context in the Gospel of Mark. The verses that immediately precede this little story are a savage warning against the scribes who love the best seats in the synagogues and who "devour widows' houses," perhaps by asking poor widows to give just a little bit more to the support of those religious houses! The passage that follows the widow's mite relativizes radically the significance of all religious structures, even the Temple to which the widow has given her little all.

> And as he came out of the temple, one of his disciples said to him, "Look, Teacher, what large stones and what large buildings!" Then Jesus asked him, "Do you see these great buildings? Not one stone will be left here upon another; all will be thrown down."

The action of the woman is still admirable; Jesus values the depth of her love and commitment. But what about those who urged her to give? Is their action equally admirable? And, thinking analogically, is this really a text we still want to use for Stewardship Sunday?

Here are a few more practice questions:

(1) What is the effect of reading Psalm 23 immediately after Psalm 22?

(2) What links the series of stories in Mark 2:1 — 3:6? Describe the progression you see there.

(3) Outline the structure of Luke, chapter 10. Why does the Martha and Mary story follow the parable of the good Samaritan?

3. What form or literary type is this passage?

Examples are parable, miracle story/tale, hymn, lament, proverb. Compare your passage to other passages of the same form. If there are variations from what seems to be the standard form, they are probably among the most significant points in your passage.

It is not always possible to identify very precisely the form of the text. Sometimes one can say little more than that the text is a "narrative" or "exhortation" or "doctrinal exposition." Where it is possible to identify the form of the text more precisely, we possess a vital clue to its meaning. One might compare the idea of interpretation that prevailed in older-style preaching to the operation of a still. A still boils away the liquid and distills from it a highly concentrated alcoholic liquor. Similarly, in interpretation everything was boiled away until a concept was identified that was the true meaning of the text. A recent version of this method calls this conceptual material the "exegetical idea," which in turn becomes the "homiletical idea."[19] But how we say something is as important in communication as what we say. The meaning of a text is not the conceptual material that is left over when the form of the text is boiled away. Rather, meaning is content expressed in form. To alter the form is to alter the meaning. Many contemporary homileticians urge the preacher to pay as much attention to the form of the text as to its content.

Contemporary homiletics has turned away from the distillation principle, the idea that one distills from the text a proposition or idea and carries that proposition across the time divide into our world. What a text does is a vital part of what it says and therefore must influence the form of the sermon.[20] "What a text does" is a question of form. To identify rightly the form of a text is also to make it possible to say what is the function of the text. So a hymn, for example, is a song in praise of God. What does a hymn do? *It praises God.*

> My soul magnifies the Lord, and my spirit rejoices in God my Savior.
>
> (Luke 1:46)

Another psalm might be identified as a lament; it *bewails* the sad lot of the individual psalmist or of the people of Israel.

> Be gracious to me, O LORD, for I am in distress;
>   my eye wastes away from grief,
>   my soul and body also.
> For my life is spent with sorrow,
>   and my years with sighing;
> my strength fails because of my misery,
>   and my bones waste away.
>
> (Ps. 31: 9–10)

There are, of course, many other identifiable forms. A Gospel pericope might be identified, for example, as a miracle story (a tale in the classification system I learned in seminary). A miracle story *tells a story* about some highly unusual and significant action, in this case of Jesus. A Bible dictionary or exegetical handbook will identify many such forms.

It is not the case, as we shall see, that a sermon can always do what the text does. A proverb, for example, expresses a truth in a short pithy statement; most would last about three seconds if spoken aloud. A sermon cannot be quite as compressed in form as a proverb! Nor does a sermon on a hymn need to be a song of praise nor a sermon on a lament a sorrowful account of one's troubles. Imagine imitating the form of Psalm 31!

> Be gracious to me, O Lord, for I am a minister;
>> my eye is wasted with exegesis
>> and my soul with sermon preparation.
> For my life is spent in committee meetings
>> and my years with the filling out of forms from the national church!

Sometimes, as we shall see, a sermon not only cannot but may not appropriately do what a text does; the imprecations against the enemies and the ungodly in the psalms may be an example of this. Would we actually wish that those who trouble us with their ungodliness should be "consumed from the earth"? But it is always appropriate to consider the form of the text and its implications for the form of the sermon. Consider a lament like Psalm 31. While a litany of complaint is in itself not the right form for the sermon material itself, a sermon on a lament should be more than a dry theological disquisition on, say, the sources of suffering. It should reach down toward the genuine depths of human suffering that we all experience. It should attempt to acknowledge and give voice to that pain. A sermon on a hymn should likewise do more than make theological assertions about God; it should rejoice and invite the congregation to share in that rejoicing. Don't forget to consider the form of the sermon!

Identifying a text's form may also enable us to identify variations from the form. If such variations are present, they are likely to be theologically and therefore homiletically significant. The best way to do this is compare the passage we are studying with other texts of the same type. Imagine that we are about to preach on Luke 9:10–17, the feeding of the five thousand. It is quite obviously a miracle story, of which there is no particular shortage in the Gospels. The simplest of all the miracle stories, and one to which it might be interesting to compare our text, is Mark 1:29–31, the healing of Simon Peter's mother-in-law.

The latter story has four elements that recur in many of the miracle stories. These are:

1. *Setting:* Simon and Andrew's house; James and John are also present with Jesus.
2. *Problem:* Simon's mother-in-law has a fever.
3. *Response:* Jesus heals her.
4. *Proof:* She rises and serves them.

Further study would show us that the first three elements are invariably present in miracle stories and the fourth is common. The proof is an action that is a little more than strictly necessary to show that the miracle has occurred. Simon's mother-in-law does not simply stretch her arms and say, "My, I feel much better! I think I could even take a little chicken soup now!" She rises and serves Jesus and the others.

The same elements are quite obviously present in the feeding of the five thousand:

1. *Setting:* Jesus is with a great crowd in a secluded place.
2. *Problem:* Hunger!
3. *Response:* Jesus feeds the crowd.
4. *Proof:* Twelve baskets of leftovers are collected.

Set out this way, what is unusual, in fact unique, about this particular miracle story is immediately obvious. There is in the middle of the story a dialogue with the disciples. They, practical realists that they are, urge Jesus to send the crowd away for food. He responds, "You give them something to eat." Is there another miracle story in which Jesus challenges the disciples in a like manner? This is something striking and unusual here! As a result of the challenge, the disciples are brought face to face with their own inadequacy. The problem is so great and their resources are so small! Let us get well ahead of ourselves here. This book is about analogical preaching, that is, a way of preaching that moves from the world of the text to the contemporary world by way of analogy. We will be looking for analogies between our world and the world of the text. The fundamental analogy from which the sermon may grow seems pretty obvious here.

It is not the case that this kind of comparison will always be fruitful. Many texts cannot be easily categorized into a particular form, and of the ones that can, many do not display significant variations. It is always worth asking the question, however. What is the form of this text? What does this text do?

PRACTICE QUESTIONS

(1) What is the form of the following texts? What do these texts do?
Psalm 22; Isaiah 5:1–7; Isaiah 5:8–30; Luke 1:68–79; 1 Corinthians 1:1–3; 1 Corinthians 1:4–9.

(2) What is unusual about the form of Luke 5:17–26?

(3) Compare the form of Matthew 5:1–11 and Luke 6:20–26.

4. What is the movement of my passage?

Draw the structure of your passage using blocks, line and circles, or other devices, and label the parts. Identify any significant rhetorical devices such as metaphors, rhetorical questions, or repetitions, and describe their function.

I used to speak here of the structure of the passage, but have come to believe that the word "structure" is too static for what occurs in a text and for what one hopes will happen in a sermon.[21] Texts have within them some kind of movement. This movement need not be spatial, from point A to point B, although spatial movements are often highly significant. The kind of movement we are searching for here is a movement from one state to another, a change in status or situation, for example. In most texts a transformation of some sort occurs; there is, as a result, some pattern within them, some movement from beginning to end. Something happens in them.

This is true even of nonnarrative texts such as doctrinal exposition or collections of laws or proverbs. Sometimes such materials are considered only abstract speculation, or arid explanations of ideas or concepts far distant from the stuff of human life. But ideas and concepts, rightly considered, are embedded in our lives. People come to ideas as the result of reflection on some experience or experiences. The grasping of a concept does something to them, or the failure to grasp a concept has certain consequences. Ideas are far from the arid intellectual counters we sometimes think them. Consider the consequences of genuinely accepting one or another of these concepts: "All people are created equal and endowed by their creator with certain inalienable rights," or "There is a master race and it is ours." There is nothing as powerful as a good idea or as dangerous as a bad one. Never underestimate ideas and never think that they are somehow divorced from ordinary life. In texts that seem to be about ideas, look for the movement they result from or cause.

As interpreters of scripture and as preachers, we need to get at those internal transformations. Preaching, after all, is about transformation; the primary aim of the gospel is not to convey information, but to effect a transformation.

The transformations that occur in the text may well be analogously related to the transformations that may occur in and among our people.

As interpreters of scripture, therefore, we must look for the verbal and rhetorical clues that point to the movement of the text and the transformations that occur within it. To ascertain these clues we will use many of the same techniques that we learned in literature classes in high school or university. We may not have been asked in those classes to draw the text, but drawing the passage may in some people engage the right side of the brain from which comes a large measure of our creativity.

This question may in certain cases lead us directly from text to sermon. Later in the book my own analysis of the movements in Luke 15:11–32, the most familiar of all Jesus' parables, together with the sermon that follows it, will appear. It may be helpful to turn to those pages to see an example of this process. Here let me deal briefly with another passage, Luke 1:46–55, Mary's Magnificat, a lovely song of praise set within Luke's infancy narrative. A student noticed that the text moves from the individual to the corporate. She was struck also by the parallelism that is so characteristic of Hebrew poetry. The result was a fascinating drawing:

	for me	people	
My	**soul**	**magnifies**
	things	for God's	
My	**spirit**	**rejoices**
	great	help	

PRACTICE QUESTIONS

(1) Outline the movement of the following passages: Genesis 18:1–15; Luke 10:25–37; 1 Corinthians 1:1–17.

(2) Draw the transformations you perceive in them.

5. How does this passage relate to other parts of scripture?

a. (For NT New Testament texts) Are there OT (Old Testament) allusions or quotations?
    If so, how does the author make use of these source materials?

b. (For OT texts) Is this material taken up in the NT?
    If so, how are these materials used in their new settings?

c. If your text is in the lectionary, why were the readings for the day put together?

d. Are there parallel passages? (This is a vital consideration for the Synoptic Gospels.)
    If so, compare your passage with its parallel(s).
    List the differences.
    Decide which ones are significant.
    Account as best you can for the differences.

Scripture is its own best interpreter. Comparison of our preaching text with other related texts is very often a useful way of grasping its theological significance. Sometimes there is an obvious relation of a text to other points in scripture. A quotation such as "All this took place to fulfill what had been spoken by the Lord through the prophet: 'Look, the virgin shall conceive and bear a son, and they shall name him Emmanuel'" is a particularly striking example. Here Matthew 1:23 quotes Isaiah 7:14. If one were preaching from Matthew's Christmas story it would be appropriate to go back to the prophetic word of Isaiah and consider what use Matthew is making of the source material. Similarly, if one were preaching from Isaiah 7 it would be necessary to consider how the New Testament takes up and alters the significance of that passage.[22] The New Testament is full of allusions to the Old Testament of varying degrees of subtlety. To uncover them is not merely an act of biblical archaeology: "Dearly beloved, we should note, first of all, that the author of the Letter to the Hebrews is here referring to a practice outlined in the book of Leviticus, with which, I am sure, we are all familiar." Rather, it is to begin to grasp after the theological significance of the passage within the world of the first audience. We know how much of our own present-day communication is a series of direct and indirect references to the web of images and stories that shape our own communal consciousness. We recognize immediately that an effective speaker in our own time appeals to those images and stories constantly. The web of images and stories that shaped the communal consciousness of the New Testament church was largely derived from their Bible, our Old Testament. Effective communicators in the early church, in particular the evangelists, did likewise. So the tedious preacher is quite right in content, if not in form of presentation; the Letter to the Hebrews is full of references to Leviticus and to many other Old Testament books, as is, with respect to the Old Testament, the case with almost every other book in the New Testament.

It is not merely that one cannot, for instance, grasp intellectually the argument of the Letter to the Hebrews without some knowledge of the sacrificial system of the Jerusalem Temple; it is that one cannot, without knowing something of that system, grasp emotionally the impact of the declaration that Jesus Christ is the great high priest who has, once and for all, made sacrifice for us. To be sure, the preacher will have to decide how much of that web of images and stories must be re-created in the sermon and how it may be done without inducing terminal ennui. But one cannot even begin to consider that question until at least some of the images and stories have been identified.

If one is preaching from an Old Testament text that is quoted or alluded to in the New, the matter is even more complex. "When Israel was a child, I loved him, and out of Egypt I called my son," writes Hosea (Hos. 11:1), speaking for a God who weeps over the unfaithfulness of a covenant people. A premature move to the New Testament use of such a text prevents us from hearing this word in its original setting. In this particular case, Matthew quotes Hosea 1 and renders it as a prediction of the flight of the Holy Family into Egypt, surely a substantial shift in the meaning of the text. But a Christian congregation can profitably understand the coming of Jesus in terms of the love that will not let even an unfaithful and adulterous people depart, that will give anything to claim that people back. The extent of that "anything" that God will give is made all the more poignant when we hear the anguish of parental love in Hosea 11.[23] If a preacher's desire is that the congregation may grasp with mind and heart the whole story of scripture and not simply small episodes thereof, an eventual move to the New Testament may well be justified and even necessary. The question of whether and when the preacher should move from an Old Testament pericope into the New Testament is a vigorously debated one. I cannot pretend to solve the problem here, but it does seem to me that where the Old Testament text is taken up in the New, the preacher may have a responsibility to deal with the relationship.[24] The canon of scripture as a whole is the literary and theological context of a text in either Testament. To move from one testament to the other is not to move out of a passage's context.

If we are using the lectionary, it is also vital to consider why the framers placed the particular texts for the day together. Is there some particular theological theme or concern that binds these texts in one? Remember that the new context supplied by placing these texts together may subtly or even crudely alter the way the texts are heard by the people in the congregation. If you conclude that the alteration is so serious that it constitutes a misrepresentation of the text, you may have to take steps to counteract the effect of reading the texts together.

If there is a parallel version of the preaching text, as is often the case in the Gospels, it is usually enlightening to compare the text with its parallels. This, by the way, is sometimes a stimulating activity in a Bible study group, such as the ones some ministers convene to study the lectionary texts each week. The process is relatively simple: Lay the texts side by side. List the differences and decide which are significant. (Some aren't; they are simply different ways of saying much the same thing.) Account as best as you can for the differences that are theologically significant. Some church members, and indeed some clergy, have a desire to harmonize the Gospel accounts, to minimize or gloss over the differences between the Gospels. This attitude is, I believe, a mistake; differences between the evangelists' accounts are signposts to meaning.

Sometimes the comparison reveals fascinating tidbits about the text. Sometimes the comparison lets us grasp theological concerns of first importance. For example, a comparison of Mark 2:1–12, the story of the healing of the paralytic let down through the roof, with its parallels shows that Mark is prepared to identify the house. "It was reported that he [Jesus] was *at home*" (italics added). Can you imagine the chutzpah of the friends, digging a hole in Jesus' roof, peering down as if to say, "But could you do a favor for our friend?" What is *chutzpah?* Chutzpah is when a man murders his father and mother then throws himself on the mercy of the court because he is an orphan. It was chutzpah indeed, but Jesus sees something else. "And when Jesus saw their faith . . . " Perhaps faith is not so much an invisible attitude as something that can be seen. Perhaps faith and chutzpah are more closely related than we had thought. Note also that it is the friends' faith that is noted, not that of the paralytic. We have no evidence whatever with respect to the attitude of the paralytic. Perhaps the faith of others can be of immense significance in the work of God?

PRACTICE QUESTIONS

(1) Identify and consider the significance of the Old Testament allusions in Luke 4:16–30.

(2) How is Psalm 8: 4–6 used in Hebrews 2:6–9?

(3) Compare the following texts: Luke 14:15–24 and Matthew 22:1–10; Matthew 14:13–21, Mark 6:30–44, Luke 9:10–17, and John 6:1–14.

What is the particular significance of each individual text?

6. How does this passage fit into the history of its time?

Outline briefly the historical circumstances surrounding the events described in your passage and/or the period of its composition.

To discover the answer to this question was in former times a chief aim of exegesis. In a sense, the older criticism was an essentially historical discipline; it is noteworthy that the German term *Geschichte,* which is usually rendered "criticism" in translation, actually means "history." Newer forms of criticism, on the other hand, owe more to literary studies. Our interest is not confined to events behind the text; meaning can be found in the text and is created in front of the text in the interaction between text and reader/listener. But to say that the focus of interest has shifted is not to say that the history out of which the text has grown is of no interest whatever.[25]

Consider Psalm 137: "By the rivers of Babylon—there we sat down and there we wept when we remembered Zion." Who are "we"? What are they doing in Babylon? Why are they weeping? Who are the "captors" who say to them, "Sing us one of the songs of Zion!"? Surely any treatment of the text, even one that intends to create an experience rather than to convey information, must depend on the answer to such questions. What is true of Psalm 137 is true of many other texts, particularly in the Old Testament.

It is not true, however, of all texts. In some cases the historical background cannot be specified with any confidence. And speculative reconstructions of the "real" historical circumstances behind a text are of little use for preaching. A particularly striking example is Hans Conzelmann's contention that behind the parable of the good Samaritan lies a discussion in the early church concerning the place of Samaritan Christians.[26] Such a theory is hypothetical at best and homiletically useless in any case. In other cases the text springs from and speaks of realities that are, if not exactly timeless, at least perennial. Many of the psalms and virtually all the proverbs fall into this category. What is the historical background of Psalm 23 or Psalm 100? Do we know? And would it matter if we did?

Even here, however, historical background is not completely irrelevant and useless. In our day the term "Samaritan" is an honorable one. For example, the main inner-city mission in my city of Toronto publishes a "Good Samaritan Corner" weekly in the newspapers in order to keep its donors informed of its activities. Among first-century Jews the name was not held in such high esteem. Jews and Samaritans hated each other. At some earlier time, Samaritans had dumped a load of pig bones in the Temple precincts as a sign of that contempt. The emotional impact of the story is lessened if the hearers are unaware of that historical background of mutual prejudice. In fact, most clergy and many church members know all this about Samaritans, but very few texts are as familiar as this one. With texts such as these, at least some historical information may be not only useful but necessary.

In many cases texts were composed or compiled a considerable time after the time of the events they recount. So Deuteronomy describes events during the desert wandering between the exodus and the conquest, perhaps the thirteenth century B.C.E. Many scholars, however, argue that it was compiled in the seventh or even sixth century B.C.E. The social setting of one era is markedly different from the other! For analogical preaching the difference is highly significant. I will take up this question at greater length later in the book.

The time scale is not so great with respect to the New Testament; we are speaking of decades, not centuries, but the gap between event and event recording is still significant. The historical background of a particular pericope in a Gospel may not be only the life of the historical Jesus in Palestine ca. A.D. 30, but also the life of a Christian congregation somewhere in the diaspora ca. A.D. 85. So the warning against claiming greatness for oneself (Mark 9:33–37 and parallels) is not just a reflection of personal rivalry and excessive ambition among the disciples; it may also have been intended to combat a very real problem among the leadership of the early church. This problem is not entirely unknown in modern churches; note the possibility of a useful analogy here.

Older forms of historical criticism tried to set texts within a history of theological or ecclesiastical development. More recent scholarship has also made use of the skills of the sociologist or the social anthropologist, often with fruitful results.

Many of us will need more "expert" help with this question than with any of the others.

PRACTICE QUESTION

    (1) Identify the historical background of: Isaiah 7:10–25; Jeremiah 28:1–17; Luke 16:1–9; Titus 1:5–9.

7. How do different translations handle my passage?

Compare the rendering of your passage in three translations of different types.

> List the differences that are significant.
> Account as best you can for those differences.

Ministers and priests ought to possess translations of several different types. All translations attempt to achieve two all but mutually exclusive goals: they seek to render a text as accurately as possible and to produce a text that is vigorous and even elegant. Translations may be placed along a continuum, of which the two ends may be labeled formal and dynamic. Formal translations attempt to approximate a word-for-word translation of the text. (It is impossible to do so completely; the result of such an effort would be almost incomprehensible in English.) The RSV and NRSV are examples of this type. Dynamic translations, on the other hand, attempt to produce a thought-for-thought translation of the original. The TEV (or *Good News Bible*) is an example of this type of translation. One might want to extend the continuum beyond the dynamic translations to the category of paraphrase. Here strict accuracy tends to be sacrificed in favor of vigor of English expression. A good paraphrase can be very useful to the preacher. A generation ago the Phillips version was widely popular. Now, many pastors make use of *The Message,* a paraphrase by Eugene Peterson.

    Translations may also be classified according to the theological stream that produced them. All translations are inescapably shaped by the theological and ideological concerns of the translators. So the NIV (New International Version) is an evangelical translation, the *Living Bible* an evangelical/fundamentalist paraphrase, the NRSV a production of scholars of the so-called mainline churches; the *Jerusalem Bible* (JB) and the *New Jerusalem Bible* (NJB) are Roman Catholic versions; and the *Inclusive Language Lectionary* is a feminist rendering. The *New English Bible* (NEB) and *Revised English Bible* (REB) are markedly British rather than American, though this is hardly an ideological or theological tendency in itself!

A student once answered the question we are considering using the King James Bible, the RSV, and the NRSV. These versions, since they are really mother, daughter, and granddaughter in the history of translation, are not distinct enough to be truly useful in this exercise. The value of the exercise is lost if the versions are too similar. Clergy ought to make use of at least three versions of *different types*. One should be a formal translation and one should come from a theological stream different from one's own.

With respect to this question, it is vital to exercise some degree of judgment about what matters. Never confuse activity with achievement![27] Listing trivial variations among versions that are little more than different ways of saying much the same thing is a waste of precious time. Concentrate only on differences that appear to be theologically significant.

Consider, for example, John 1:12–13 in the NRSV: "But to all who received him, who believed in his name, he gave power to become children of God, who *were* born, not of blood or of the will of the flesh or of the will of man, but of God" (italics added). By contrast, the *Jerusalem Bible* reads in part, " . . . who *was* born not out of human stock, or urge of the flesh or will of man but of God himself" (italics added). This is pretty clearly a theologically significant difference! The NRSV speaks of the spiritual birth of believers; the *Jerusalem Bible* appears to proclaim the virgin birth of the Redeemer. In this case the two translations are following different underlying texts; the difference in number exists in the original Greek. But inasmuch as the textual support for the plural, that is, the RSV reading, is so very much stronger than for the singular, it may be that theological concerns are also at work here. The doctrine of the virgin birth may have been more highly prized among the Roman Catholic circles who produced the *Jerusalem Bible* than among the mainline Protestants who were responsible for the NRSV.[28]

It is certainly not the case that we will always find differences as interesting and significant as this in our preaching texts, but it is always worth checking. Sometimes even a difference in emphasis that is produced by the various translations can be theologically and homiletically stimulating. One further point: Read the translations *aloud* while doing this exercise.

PRACTICE QUESTIONS

(1) Examine Isaiah 7:14 in the King James Version, the *Jerusalem Bible,* the NIV, and the NRSV.

(2) What is the theological significance of the translation difference you find there?

8. What are the key words or phrases in my passage?

Key words or phrases are likely to be those that:

> are repeated
> occur at key junctures in the passage
> are points of contact with other parts of the Bible
> reflect significant differences between translations

Explain the significance of these words or phrases.

Even if you have not translated the passage, you will profit if you look up these words in a lexicon or theological dictionary.

A community that loses its language will probably die. By language I do not mean a separate tongue such as English, French, or Swahili; I mean a characteristic way of speaking about reality couched in a particular vocabulary, used in ways that are widely accepted in an identifiable community. The Christian church is an identifiable community with its own commonly shared vocabulary. If Christians lose that vocabulary, the church may well die or at least change beyond recognition. Historically, that vocabulary has been largely drawn from the scriptures. With the decline of biblical literacy among our members and even among our clergy, that vocabulary may be in danger of being lost—a loss we simply cannot afford.

Moreover, the relationship between language and experience is not nearly so simple as we might first think. Yale theologian George Lindbeck has argued that what he calls the experiential-expressive view of the role of language is not an adequate description of reality. In this view human beings have certain experiences and then find language to express the experience. Human experiences, including religious experiences, are in essence the same whatever language is used to express them. Lindbeck, by contrast, argues that it is at least as much the case that a particular language enables us to have particular experiences.[29] It at least seems to me true that if we do not possess the language to describe a particular experience we will not be able to recognize such an experience when it does happen to us. And is an unrecognized experience an experience in any meaningful sense of the word?

Imagine two neighbors: Neighbor A becomes a member of a charismatic religious community that speaks frequently of "miracles" and the "hand of the Lord." She will likely have experiences that she will interpret as miraculous. She will tell any inquirer that experience corroborates the theology of her group. Neighbor B, on the other hand, has a loose connection to a more liberal church, which avoids such language "religiously." She will not have "miraculous" experiences and may well doubt the reality of the experiences of which neighbor A speaks.

What will happen to a church that loses its biblical vocabulary? If Lindbeck is even partially correct, it may lose biblical experiences. If, for example, we no longer speak of salvation, will we experience it? We preachers need to reclaim for ourselves and for our people a Christian vocabulary.

We can do this by using and explaining the key words of the Christian faith. Let me introduce a distinction here between Christian vocabulary and Christian jargon. Christian jargon in one church might include language such as "beseech" instead of "ask," or "bestow" rather than "give." It may be marked by the use of the archaic second person singular, "thee and thou," and a strange fondness for verbs in the subjunctive mood. A prayer in such a church might begin, "We beseech thee, O God, that thou wouldst bestow upon us . . . " Another sort of jargon, in a rather different church, might produce a different prayer: "Wejis wanna ask you, Jesus . . . " There is no real holiness in using words like bestow or sprinkling our prayers with that strange formulation "wejis" (as if prayer were some small minor thing!). On the other hand, words like "grace," "covenant," "salvation," "glory" are, in my opinion, vital to the Christian vocabulary and therefore to Christian life. It is not only in *Reader's Digest* that it pays to increase our word power!

We can do so by examining a maximum of three words or phrases per week. After a period of time we will have an extensive working vocabulary of the Bible. There is little that is more truly useful to the busy preacher and leader of Bible studies than this knowledge. Remember that most of these terms keep recurring in our texts. Imagine the usefulness of being able to look at a text, perhaps for the first time, and having something worthwhile "in the bank" to say about a key word in that text!

The key words in a passage, as we pointed out, are likely to be those that are repeated, that occur at key junctures in the structure of the passage, are points of contact with other parts of scripture, or are handled differently by the translations. In addition, some words just simply carry more theological weight. Use a concordance to discover interesting uses of the same word elsewhere in the Bible. Pay particular attention to the use of the word or phrase elsewhere in the same book or by the same author. Note carefully: Be sure you know what word is used in the original Greek or Hebrew! Remember that the same English word may be used to render several different words in the original. Most concordances group words according to their originals; be sure to make use of this valuable tool. Bible dictionaries are also extremely valuable resources here.

But back to this matter of words, of vital words. One of those words is "glory." We use the word or its verbal form "glorify" regularly in church, but without any clear notion of what it means. We might remember the Christmas story, "And the glory of the Lord shone round about them" (Luke 2:9, KJV) and think it means a bright light. But would we really understand the angels in the same story to mean "Bright lights to God in the highest"? In fact, the word goes back to the Hebrew verb "to be heavy"; it means "weight." Suddenly we can begin to grasp its meaning. Perhaps in ancient times the largest, heaviest man in a tribe was the most obvious choice for chief. The "chief" may well not be heavy these days, or even a man, but the notion behind the word is by no means foreign to us. We say, "Her word carries weight," or "He's a real heavyweight." To give God glory is to claim that, despite all appearances to the contrary, the real "heavyweight" in our universe is not the head of a multinational corporation or the President of the United States, but God. It is to confess that for us God's word carries weight![30] Words, even words that we use so often we have forgotten their meaning, *words matter!*

PRACTICE QUESTIONS

   (1) What are the key words in Micah 6:1–8; Mark 8:34—9:1; Ephesians 2:1–10?

   (2) Explain the significance of the word "poor" in Luke 6:20.

9. What is unusual, striking, perhaps even offensive to contemporary ears about this passage?

In analogical preaching we are looking for a point of intersection between the world of the text and our own world. To base the sermon on a fundamental analogy presupposes that there will be more similarity than difference between the two worlds. This may not be the case. The contemporary listener may be faced first with a sense of distance between our world and the text. She or he may be powerfully struck by something in the text that is unusual or even offensive, which may prevent the listener from perceiving any basic similarity between the worlds.

The proper response in such cases is not at all to ignore or to minimize the difficulty. Rather, one might use the strength of the objection to draw the listener into a more genuine encounter with the text. It is not unlike judo. In that sport a competitor does not so much resist the force of the opponent's attack, but rather uses its strength as the power to pull the rival off balance. Now, of course the members of a congregation are not the preacher's sporting competitors! But there is a real enemy to good preaching. The enemy of good preaching is not opposition or even emotional revulsion to the text—it is disinterest. Identifying the negative reaction and making use of it is an effective way of defeating disinterest.

There are, it must be admitted, pitfalls for the inexperienced preacher in emphasizing the negative. I remember a student in one of my first classes who was particularly impressed with my classroom advice about acknowledging and making use of the striking and even the repulsive. At some point I had discussed Luke 14, and noted how surprised I had been by what seems like rudeness in Jesus, according to our standards of etiquette. The student chose to preach on that chapter shortly thereafter in the church in which a friend of mine was pastor. The resulting sermon went something like this: In Luke 14, Jesus is very rude. Go and do thou likewise! The elders, appalled at this performance, rushed up to my friend, complained bitterly about the quality of the sermon, and asked indignantly, "Who's teaching preaching at the college these days?" My friend took particular delight in reporting the incident to me! Just how one may rightly use the problems contemporary listeners may have with a text will be taken up later in the book. For now, let me say only that making use of these negative reactions does not mean surrender to them. One may begin a sermon with the negative—one does not end there!

PRACTICE QUESTION

What is striking, unusual, or offensive about the following texts: Psalm 35; Psalm 137; Isaiah 5:1–7; Luke 14:25–33; 1 Peter 2:11–25?

10. How would I write a summary of the passage in one sentence?

It is quite true that a one-sentence summary will not adequately express the richness and depth of any passage. Nevertheless, it seems to me useful to do so in order to maintain focus and coherence throughout the process of composing the sermon. The preacher who keeps in mind a short, concise statement of what the text is about and what it does is less likely to wander about dallying with all kinds of extraneous material.

Thomas Long urges the preacher to write both a *focus* and a *function statement* as the result of the process of exegesis.[31] The distinction is a valid one; the two statements can help us to grasp both what the text is about and what it does. I prefer to seek a statement of which the focus is expressed functionally. That is to say, the focus statement should tell not only what the text is about but also what it does, so that there is no separation between the two. Thus a summary statement for the Magnificat, Luke 1:46–55, could be: "In Jesus Christ, God acts on the side of the poor and downtrodden." It would be better, however, to say, "Mary rejoices that in Jesus Christ, God acts on the side of the poor and downtrodden."

The sentence ought to be just that, a sentence. It should be grammatically complete, verb and all, but it should not bloat into a pseudo paragraph. It should be Ernest Hemingway length, not William Faulkner!

PRACTICE QUESTION
Write one-sentence summaries of any three of the texts used earlier in this chapter.

EXEGESIS OF THE TEXT

The following is an outline of a brief exegetical method useful in preparing for preaching. It does not depend on the use of the original language, although use of that language will greatly enrich the exegete's understanding of the passage under consideration.

Ask yourself the following questions *without the aid of commentaries.*

1. How much am I going to deal with?

Answering this question is necessary for purely practical reasons; considering it is also the first step toward uncovering the meaning of the passage. Some of the following subquestions may help you determine the limits of the passage:

    a.   How does the passage differ from what comes before and after it?
    b.   Is this passage a particular literary form? (See question 3.)
    c.   Does it have a coherent and complete internal structure? (See question 4.)
    d.   Is there a change in place between this passage and what surrounds it?

    e. Is there a change of characters between this passage and what surrounds it?

    f. Is there a change of subject matter between this passage and what surrounds it?

    g. Is there a repetition of a key word or phrase (*inclusio*) at the beginning and end of the passage?

    h. Is there an indicator of time at the beginning or end of this passage?

2. How does this passage fit into its literary surroundings?

What is the theological significance of the placement of this passage at this particular point?

At this point those who have a working knowledge of the original language should translate the passage.

3. What form or literary type is this passage?

Examples are parable, miracle story/tale, hymn, lament proverb.

Compare your passage to other passages of the same form. If there are variations from what seems to be the standard form, they are probably among the most significant points in your passage.

4. What is the movement of my passage?

Draw the movement of your passage using blocks, line and circles, or other devices, and label the parts. Identify any significant rhetorical devices such as metaphors, rhetorical questions, or repetitions, and describe their function.

5. How does this passage relate to other parts of scripture?
    a. (For NT texts) Are there OT allusions or quotations? If so, how does the author make use of these source materials?
    b. (For OT texts) Is this material taken up in the NT? If so, how are these materials used in their new settings?
    c. If your text is in the lectionary, why were the readings for the day put together?
    d. Are there parallel passages? (This is a vital consideration for the Synoptic Gospels.)

If so, compare your passage with its parallel(s).
List the differences.
Decide which ones are significant.
Account as best you can for the differences.

6. How does this passage fit into the history of its time?

Outline briefly the historical circumstances surrounding the events described in your passage and/or the period of its composition.

7. How do different translations handle my passage?

Compare the rendering of your passage in three translations of different types.
List the differences that are significant.
Account as best you can for those differences.

8. What are the key words or phrases in my passage?

Key words or phrases are likely to be those that:
are repeated
occur at key junctures in the passage
are points of contact with other parts of the Bible
reflect significant differences between translations
Explain the significance of these words or phrases. Even if you have not translated the passage you will profit if you look up these words in a lexicon or theological dictionary.

9. What is unusual, striking, perhaps even offensive to contemporary
ears about this passage?

10. Write a one-sentence summary of the passage.

Now that you have answered the ten questions for yourself, look at the commentaries. Run through the process a second time adding the knowledge you gain from these resources.
Write a revised one-sentence summary of the passage.

four

From Text to Sermon:
Finding the Analogies

The problem for the preacher who has got into the "exegetical habit" is not lack of information. Most preachers have enough exegetical training, if they put it to use, to gather more than enough information about a given text to create a sermon. The real difficulty lies in moving from the possession of information about the text to a proclamation of the gospel through the text. The Word, I have argued, can happen when text and contemporary world are brought together by the use of analogy. I intend in the remainder of the book to suggest a method of identifying and using analogies between the world of the text and our world. We may then use these analogies to shape the sermons we preach from the text.

What follows is an attempt to guide you through the sometimes difficult move from text to sermon. It is cast in the form of a series of steps. In actual practice, however, the steps are not discrete; they flow naturally into one another. The key methodological points are highlighted in boxes.

1. Identify the persons or groups in or behind your text.

PERSONS OR GROUPS IN THE TEXT

If your text is a narrative, the first part of this task is easy. Take, for example, the so-called parable of the prodigal son, Luke 15:11–32. The first verse of that parable tells us, "Then Jesus said, 'There was a man who had two sons.'" Clearly enough, the persons in the text are a *father*, a *younger son* and an *older son*. One could go on to name others—a foreign landowner, partygoers, the father's servants, for exam-

> Keep your focus on the main characters in your text.

ple. It is probably unwise to do so; there is a danger of becoming a little too "cute" here. There is a story of a preacher who followed this process too far and entitled a sermon "The Palm Sunday Story—As Told by an Ass." It is best to keep the focus of the sermon on the main characters.

Another example might be Luke 7:36–50. The beginning of that text tells us, "One of the Pharisees asked Jesus to eat with him, and he went into the Pharisee's house and took his place at the table. And a woman in the city, who was a sinner, having learned that he was eating in the Pharisee's house, brought an alabaster jar of ointment." Here the chief characters are *Jesus,* a *sinful woman,* and *Simon the Pharisee,* Jesus' host for the evening.

Often, however, we are dealing not simply with individuals but with a group. In Mark 2:1–12, the story of the paralytic let down through the roof, we do have individual persons, *Jesus* and

> Look for groups as well as individuals!

the *paralytic.* We also see the friends who have the faith to bring the man to Jesus, the unnamed *Pharisees* and *teachers of the law,* and the *crowd.* All are identifiable groups.

The text does not need to be a narrative, however. Consider Psalm 137:

> By the rivers of Babylon—
>   there we sat down and there we wept
>   when we remembered Zion.
> On the willows there
>   we hung up our harps.
> For there our captors
>   asked us for songs,
> and our tormentors asked for mirth, saying,
>   "Sing us one of the songs of Zion!"
>
> How could we sing the LORD's song
>   in a foreign land?
> If I forget you, O Jerusalem,
>   let my right hand wither!
> Let my tongue cling to the roof of my mouth,
>   if I do not remember you,
> if I do not set Jerusalem
>   above my highest joy.
>
> Remember, O LORD, against the Edomites
>   the day of Jerusalem's fall,
> how they said, "Tear it down! Tear it down!
>   Down to its foundations!"

> O daughter Babylon, you devastator!
>> Happy shall they be who pay you back
>> what you have done to us!
>> Happy shall they be who take your little ones
>> and dash them against the rock!

Three groups are easily identifiable in this passage: the *exiled Jews,* the *Babylonians,* and the *Edomites.*

We could also turn to the messy situation of the church in Corinth, as Paul describes it in the first chapter of First Corinthians. There verses 10–12 read:

> Now I appeal to you, brothers and sisters, by the name of our Lord Jesus Christ, that all of you be in agreement and that there be no divisions among you, but that you be united in the same mind and the same purpose. For it has been reported to me by Chloe's people that there are quarrels among you, my brothers and sisters. What I mean is that each of you says, "I belong to Paul," or "I belong to Apollos," or "I belong to Cephas," or "I belong to Christ."

In this text there are four factions in the church. Three have lined themselves up behind popular preachers, *Paul, Peter,* and *Apollos;* one is a spiritual party that claims to belong to *Christ alone. "Chloe's people"* are also an identifiable group. In the book as a whole, there appear in the text *Paul the apostle* himself and his fellow evangelists on the one hand, and the turbulent *church of Corinth* on the other. At their worst, the Corinthians are a collection of drunks, sex fiends, and argumentative troublemakers. Oddly enough, Paul also calls them saints. It is this *troubled church* that is the chief character or group in the text here and throughout the letter.[1] The Corinthians, the factions in their church, and Paul himself can be readily identified as groups in this text.

PERSONS OR GROUPS
BEHIND THE TEXT

Some knowledge of the literary and historical situation of the text is a must when identifying persons or groups behind the text. Consider, for example, Deuteronomy 6:20–25, fine homiletical material:

> When your children ask you in time to come, "What is the meaning of the decrees and the statutes and the ordinances that the LORD our God has commanded you?" then you shall say to your children, "We were Pharaoh's slaves in Egypt, but the LORD brought us out of Egypt with a

mighty hand. The LORD displayed before our eyes great and awesome signs and wonders against Egypt, against Pharaoh and all his household. He brought us out from there in order to bring us in, to give us the land that he promised on oath to our ancestors. Then the LORD commanded us to observe all these statutes, to fear the LORD our God, for our lasting good, so as to keep us alive, as is now the case. If we diligently observe this entire commandment before the LORD our God, as he has commanded us, we will be in the right."

It is not hard to identify the persons and groups in this text: *parents, children,* and the *Israelites* whom Moses is addressing. This text, with respect to its place in Deuteronomy's narrative, is part of Moses' final words to the children of Israel, his last will and testament. To the desert-hardened warriors of the people and to their families he gives his final instructions, including this command to rehearse to the children in years to come the mighty acts of God. After Moses' death the tribes pour into the fertile lands of Canaan and wrest it from the inhabitants. This may have taken place about 1200 B.C.E.

There is another group, which is not in the text but behind the text, however, for there is always a story behind the story. These people live in the seventh century B.C.E. In their time the faith is old and in many eyes discredited. The power of Assyria is great, and its gods are popular. Even the king on the throne, though a descendant of David, is an enthusiastic collaborator named Manasseh. Manasseh worships the foreign idols and, indeed, has sacrificed his son to those strange gods. All the great days of Israel seem surely as dead as a past which many are eager to forget. Israel's God seems powerless or nonexistent. Most certainly, the future does not seem to be with that God, and it is terribly hard to hang on to the young people. Some priests, perhaps from the old Northern Kingdom, long disappeared, collected the old laws and wrote a new book, a second law,[2] for a people in desperate need of renewal. These people, the *struggling faithful,* imperial *Assyria,* and *willing collaborators,* are behind this and any text in Deuteronomy.

> There are always more characters than appear on the surface of the biblical story. Look behind the text too!

Similarly, in the texts from the Gospel of Luke quoted above there are more characters than appear on the surface of the story. Consider again, for example, the so-called "prodigal son." Luke tells us who are the people against whom the parables of Luke 15 are aimed: "Now all the tax collectors and sinners were coming near to listen to him. And the Pharisees and the scribes were grumbling and saying, 'This fellow welcomes sinners and eats with them.' So he told them this parable" (Luke 15:1–3).

On the first level there are the characters in the parable itself. But the parable is a "story within a story." It serves a function within the wider narrative that is the Gospel of Luke as a whole. Beyond the parable, therefore, are the *Pharisees* and *scribes* who are its targets. They, in turn, are characters in the wider narrative of Luke. Finally, there are the people for whom Luke is writing, people like "most excellent Theophilus," who need to apprehend the gospel in an "orderly" way (Luke 1:1–4). These people live in the last quarter of the first century A.D., perhaps about the year 85. They are in all likelihood Gentiles, living in, perhaps, Syria. Most important, they are members of or connected with an early church. Perhaps a table will be helpful:

Level	Location	Characters or Groups
Characters in the parable	Parable	Father, two sons
Characters in Luke's Gospel	Gospel	Pharisees, scribes, sinners
Hearers/readers of the Gospel	History	Theophilus, Luke's church

There is further complexity—or, rather, richness of possibility—when an Old Testament text is taken up in the New Testament. Let us return to Deuteronomy 6 briefly. There we read the magnificent words of the Shema Yisrael: "Hear, O Israel: The LORD is our God, the LORD alone. You shall love the LORD your God with all your heart, and with all your soul, and with all your might."

These words are taken up in the New Testament at various points, including Luke 10:27, the introduction to the parable of the good Samaritan. The various levels now might include those identified both for Deuteronomy and for Luke. A table might again be helpful:

Level	Location	Characters or Groups
Deuteronomy	Old Testament narrative	Moses, the children of Israel
Deuteronomy's first audience	History, ca. 7th century B.C.	Faithful but troubled Israelites
Characters in Luke's Gospel	Luke's narrative	Jesus and the lawyer
Luke's first hearers/readers	History, ca. A.D. 85	Theophilus, Luke's church

All these are possible persons or groups who may be identified.

It should be noted how often this exercise turns up identifiable groups rather than merely individuals. This should not be surprising to anybody who is not trapped in late-twentieth-century Western individualism. Most of the Bible is not written primarily for individuals alone, but rather for people who have their identity through social groupings. Put simply, the Bible was not written for individual persons. Rather, the Old Testament was written for the people of Israel and the New Testament was written for the church. This, as we shall see later, can have significant consequences for our preaching.

2. Consider how we are like and how we are unlike those persons or groups. In what ways are we similar to those persons or groups? In what ways different?

These two questions are inseparable and cannot be considered apart from each other. One is not more important than the other, though in any analogical approach to the text the question of similarity must be the prior one. As we begin to answer these questions the sermon may well begin to take shape for us. Certainly, we will already be considering political, social, economic, and above all theological realities as the world of the text and our world are brought together.

In some of the cases discussed above we have identified persons in the text, in others groups. It is probably wise to search for analogies between equivalents. That is to say, if we have identified persons in the text we should look first for analogies between those persons and persons in the modern world. If we have identified groups within or behind the text, we ought to seek first analogies between those groups and groups in the contemporary world.[3]

Here are a few examples:

The World of the Text	The World in Which We Live
Israel	The church
Babylonians	Unjust power structures
The priest, the Levite, and the Samaritan	Listeners as individuals
The disciples	The church? or individual Christians?

This is by no means an exhaustive list of possible contemporary analogues. Sometimes, for example, one might consider the nation rather than the church to be the contemporary analogue of Israel. It is the case, however, that most Old Testament texts treat Israel primarily as a people with a covenant relationship to a holy God rather than as a political entity. As such the church is, I believe, a nearer equivalent than the modern secular nation. In some cases the contemporary analogue is a corporate body or group; in other cases it is an individual or individuals. Often, the decision between individual or group interpretation should be fairly obvious—the choice is, as it were, made by the text. Sometimes, a choice must made by the preacher.

At this point certain theological or ideological predispositions within the preacher come particularly strongly into play. (There is no point at which these predispositions cease to operate!) Many preachers, particularly in our individualistic society, tend to speak most easily and naturally about the individual and his or her concerns. The tendency to make corporate texts speak to individual concerns is a widespread and very dangerous one. This is how the biblical message of justice is often subverted in our churches. Others tend to speak more readily of social or corporate concerns. There is a tendency, no more than a tendency, for these predispositions to separate along "party lines" in theology, with conservatives tending toward the individual and liberals toward the collective in their preferred approaches. This is by no means a fixed rule, however. A preacher influenced heavily by Rudolf Bultmann's existential exegesis or by various psychological approaches, pop or otherwise, may be anything but theologically conservative and yet tend to speak first of individuals. Some very conservative preachers, on the other hand, will speak at length of society as a whole (usually of its failings!).

The point at issue is that if the preacher has a strong tendency to preach individualistic sermons, that person will probably all but automatically see analogies between groups or individuals in the text and individual persons in the modern world. The opposite is also true. Let me declare my bias at this point. I find unremittingly individualistic or unremittingly social preaching tedious and, worse, unbiblical. Preachers who predictably wind each text round to an evangelistic call to the altar or a harangue against American foreign policy commit the cardinal sin of causing boredom, at least in this listener!

This is not at all to say that preaching ought not to critique government policy and still less that the preacher ought not to announce the good news of God's love in Christ Jesus and call the people to put their trust in that

Savior. It is simply that the analogical approach to preaching, and indeed any other approach, is terribly vulnerable to people with an ideological or theological ax to grind. They will see the kind of analogies they want to see, the ones that will serve their program. Most of us, however, can take warning and are capable of some degree of self-analysis.[4]

The point is not that every sermon should be a balance between the individual and the corporate, but that the "preaching" of a church should be balanced over a period of time. It would certainly be a healthy exercise for preachers to go over their work for six months or a year and classify sermons as individual- or group-oriented. The results of such a survey would, in all probability, be very revealing.[5] The Bible speaks both to a holy people, Israel, and the church, and to the deepest needs and profoundest joys of the individual. Preaching that seeks to be truly biblical will do likewise. With respect to a particular sermon, I believe the text itself should direct us toward an individual or a corporate interpretation.

> The text itself should direct us toward an individual or a corporate interpretation.

It is possible to move from groups in the text to individuals in the contemporary world or vice versa, but one should do so quite consciously and with considerable care. A possible progression would be:

> Move between corporate and individual analogies only with great care!

A. Group in the text
B. Group in the contemporary world (e.g., the church)
C. The individual in the contemporary world (e.g., the individual Christian)

Between B and C there might appear a transition sentence such as "What is true for the church is also true for the individual Christian." Needless to say, it would be vital to consider carefully whether or not such a statement would be accurate!

SAMPLE TEXTS

Psalm 137

When we looked at Psalm 137, we identified three groups, the *exiled Israelites,* the *Babylonians*, and the *Edomites*. From the viewpoint of the Israelites, perhaps there were only two groups, the Israelites themselves on the one hand and the Babylonian oppressors and their allies on the other. At any rate, the distinction between Babylonians and Edomites is not as sharp as the distinction between Israelites and Babylonians.

The Israelites. We begin the process by recalling what our exegesis of the text and our other study have told us about these three groups. It seems natural to consider first the exiled Israelites. We have learned from our previous study that the psalm was written by exiles in Babylon. The Babylonians had removed from their homes the political and intellectual leadership of Israel. These people were a religious community in exile. There had been several such forced removals. From the victims of these successive exiles the foundations of their lives—their land, home, perhaps the family structure, and their Temple—had

> Begin with the knowledge of the persons or groups in the text that you have gained in your exegesis.

been torn away. Moreover, there was a connection in people's minds between the status and success of a people and the stature and power of their God. They lived therefore in a state of religious crisis. Marduk, the god of the Babylonians, must surely be the one with the power and Yahweh, their God, well, what power did Yahweh possess? The bitterness of the sorrow these people felt was palpable in the images of the psalm: "How could we sing the LORD's song in a foreign land?" We know from other sources that they speculated about the reason for their suffering. Some saw their anguish as punishment for their forebears' sins. "The fathers have eaten sour grapes, and the children's teeth are set on edge," they cried out bitterly (Jer. 31:29, Ez. 18:2). (There is another interesting little detail in the text about the exiles: apparently their captors liked their music.)

Perhaps the most striking thing about the exiles, however, is that at least some of them were filled with violent hatred. They called on God to remember the perfidy of the Edomites, and for the Babylonians they wished only the most horrible of fates. "Happy shall they be who take your little ones and dash them against the rock!" This is so horrible an image that in many cases these last verses are excised from the effective text of the psalm. Only the first six verses with their lovely poetry filled with nostalgic longing are read and preached from. This is the *hermeneutic of avoidance,* one of the most widely practiced hermeneutics in the contemporary church. I cannot advocate this hermeneutic, however, here or anywhere. In a world filled with hatred, a good deal of it religious, can we really afford to ignore hatred when we see it in the text?[6] "Ostrich" preachers who stick

their heads in the sand and refuse to face trouble in the text and in the world
are of very little use.

We are now ready for the pair of questions, How are we like, and how
are we unlike the groups in the text? The question immediately arises,
"What 'we' are we talking about here?" In other words, to what modern
persons or groups will we compare the Israelites? Since the text speaks not
of individuals but of groups, we will want
to consider groups in the modern world
rather than individuals. Normally, there
are three main possibilities here—the
Christian church, the nation, or our culture. In special circumstances there are
other possibilities. When preaching to a
gathering of the clergy, the "we" might be "we ministers or priests."
Preaching to, for example, a judicatory in a denomination, the answer
might be "we Methodists or we Presbyterians." The first three apply in
most circumstances, however.

> To what modern persons
> or groups will we
> compare the persons
> or groups in or behind
> the text?

One can state the case a little more strongly. The most significant analogue is very likely to be the church. The texts that we are reading and
preaching from were spoken to, written for, and preserved by religious
communities. The church is the religious community that now honors those
texts as scripture. It is in church that we are doing the reading and preaching, and it is the church that calls us and, lest we forget, pays us to interpret those texts. The church is the first analogue to the people of God to
whom the text is addressed. By the way, this is the analogue that I myself
would be most tempted to overuse.

At the same time, any church that is not wholly sectarian and other-
worldly will be involved with nation and world. In any congregation that
is not the gathering of a cult (in the contemporary sense of that word), the
worshipers will have to live in nation and world. The text can and often
must speak powerfully to nation and world as well.

How then are we the church like the Israelite exiles? First, we are religious people too, a community of those who believe. Moreover, we in fact
believe in the same God of justice and
love. The reality or even the appearance of
suffering, especially suffering beyond our
apparent deserving, is a genuine spiritual
problem for us. We are also, in Western
culture, a religious community in some de-
gree of trouble. Only a religious Pollyanna would deny that the influence

> How are we like the first
> person or group we have
> identified in or behind
> the text?

of Christianity in our culture has diminished markedly over the last few generations. A nineteenth-century English poet, Matthew Arnold, compared faith to the tide ebbing on Dover Beach. The tide has been flowing out for a good many decades. Many of us in the clergy, and most certainly the members of our churches, have come to feel like strangers in what psychically and spiritually used to be our own land. So many landmarks have disappeared; so many standards of belief and behavior that stood for so long have been overthrown! And with the decline of the stature of the church we begin to wonder about the power of our God. People do still like our music, by the way. Walking through the mall at Christmastime, you can hear the Salvation Army band or the loudspeaker playing "Adeste Fideles." It is true that they play it in order to put us in a buying mood, and they play it side by side with "Frosty the Snowman," but they still do like our music.

If we are like the exiles in all these respects, perhaps we are like them also in one other way that we don't want to acknowledge. We have the capacity to hate and to hate bitterly. Is there any hatred like unto religious hatred? Ask the residents of Belfast or Bosnia! Ask Salman Rushdie, if you can find him. For that matter, ask the people in many of our congregations across the country. How many of them have been torn apart by every imaginable form of dissension, and how soon that dissension turns into vile hatred. I remember visiting a troubled church on behalf of the presbytery in which it was located. One elder in the church looked at me with bewildered eyes and said, "We never have this kind of trouble in Rotary." With all due respect to Rotary Clubs, they do not reach into the depths of the soul the way religions do, and so the terrible things that dwell in those depths only rarely find their way out. And if we are appalled, and rightly so, by the hatred in the text, perhaps we should likewise be appalled by the possibility of hatred in ourselves—and be warned.

However, the case is not simply that we are like the Israelite exiles. In many ways we are unlike them. We in our North American churches include many and varied sorts of human beings. In some congregations there are indeed refugees and exiles, but we also include wealthy and influential members. Most of our members are, we must remember, citizens of the United States or

> How are we unlike the first person or group we have identified in or behind the text?

Canada, rich and powerful nations. While the Christian church has certainly diminished in significance within our society over the generations, there are still many highly influential Christian people in every area of national life. Many North American Christians "belong" here and can sing "America the Beautiful" or "O Canada" with joyful hearts. Such people do not sing the Lord's song in a strange land, but in one that is very familiar and very powerful.

The Babylonians. The last word leads us naturally to the next possibility, that we are like the Babylonians. Babylon was the great imperial power of the region in that time, exercising military and economic hegemony over the entire Fertile Crescent. The Babylonians had destroyed Jerusalem within the past half century and had carried the Israelites in exile to what is now Iraq. The analogy is obvious, but the link here is not primarily to the church but to the Western society in which the church dwells, and even to the United States in particular. Western society as a whole exercises the power in our contemporary time that the Babylonians exercised in the psalmist's time. In particular, the United States as the "sole remaining superpower" is the equivalent to Babylon. Lest we forget, there are even a goodly number of cities that the Western powers have laid waste in the last half century.

> Repeat the process with respect to other significant persons or groups in or behind the text.

In the text the most obvious characteristic of the Babylonians is that they are hated by their victims. The somber question is inescapable: "Are we too hated by our victims?" If we are able for a moment to lay aside wishful thinking, surely we shall sense the answer. There are indeed those who hate us, for what we have done and for what we have and for what we are. The hatred may be mixed with envy, and even from time to time with a reluctant admiration, but it is there. There may even be some who hate us enough to take our infants' heads and . . . Actually, what surprises me when I look at the world scene is not that such hatred exists, but that there is not more of it.

The Edomites. This is not, of course, the whole story. Our society and our actions are also unlike the Babylonians in genuinely significant ways. Before turning over the coin, however, it might be good to consider the third party, the Edomites. The Edomites were inhabitants of the Negev region in the southern part of what is the modern state of Israel. The Edomites had long nourished antagonism against the Jews. This antagonism sprang at least in part from the fact that the Edomites had themselves been the victims of Israelite expansionism in a time of Israelite power and prosperity. (Surely one historical verity is beginning already to emerge from this study.) From the point of view of the exiles, however, the most significant thing about the Edomites was that they had "cheered on" the Babylonians and had profited from the destruction of the city of Jersalem.

This strikes home to me as a Canadian. We in the Great White North like to dissociate ourselves from Americans when it is convenient to us to do so. (American readers who have traveled abroad can't have missed the red-maple-leaf flag pins every Canadian traveler sports in the most obvious location possible. Canadians do this so they won't be mistaken for Americans.) It is particularly convenient not to be American when the United States exercises its military or economic power in some questionable way. We Canadians don't take part—there aren't any recently ruined cities on our collective conscience—but some of us cheer the Americans on and most certainly, like the Edomites, we generally profit from the destruction. This is true even of Canadians who are most pious in their denunciations of American power. We remain members in good standing of the Western society of which the United States is the leader. This may not be an exclusively Canadian phenomenon, even in North America. Do certain American groups who perceive themselves to be in some way apart from the mainstream of American life and its exercise of power imitate Canadians—and Edomites—in this respect? I leave that to Americans to decide for themselves. At this point, however, we have strayed from the main point: the Edomites too are hated by their victims.

Up to this point we have merely entered a cycle of victimization, and hatred, hatred and victimization, with no apparent escape. Perhaps those who exegete by excision, simply ignoring the end of this psalm, are correct! Let it only be said that this cycle of victimization and hatred is part of our world too. Psalm 137, as a whole and uncensored, is one of the most realistic of the psalms. To censor out the hatred is to censor out reality, and a gospel that cannot deal with reality is a gospel that's not worth preaching. If we can ever suggest an escape from this cycle, that truly will be Good News. We shall return later to this problem.

It is not only the case that the United States is somewhat similar to Babylon and Canada to Edom. It is also true that we are unlike those nations. As far as I know, Babylon felt no ethical discomfort in connection with its exercise of power. There is no evidence that there were ever demonstrations against the "Israelite" war, or posters saying "Hands off Jerusalem!" In our societies, on the other hand, most attempts to exercise power produce vigorous ethical debate over the rightness or wrongness of the attempts. It is at least possible, if not always likely,[7] that our nations will act according to certain ideals to which we profess to adhere, rather than merely according to our self-interest. I believe that the presence of those ideals is connected to the influence of the Christian church, but that is not a chief concern here. Suffice it to say that this discomfort with raw power may differentiate us from the Babylonians and point us in an at least slightly more hopeful direction.

A key methodological point should be noted here. *We may already be well on our way to the sermon as it will be preached.* The kind of sermon that grows from this sort of analogical thinking will consist largely of a careful description of persons or groups in the biblical world and persons or groups in our world. We engage in this description so that our listeners will grasp and accept the fundamental analogies that we as preachers are drawing. It is in this way that the biblical text can function as a mirror of identity, showing us our own true faces in God's sight.

> The analogical sermon, as it is preached, will describe both the persons or groups in or behind the text and their analogues in our world.

Luke 7: 36–50

Not all texts have to do with groups. Consider, for example, the fascinating text Luke 7:36–50. Earlier we identified three main characters in the story, *the sinful woman, Simon the Pharisee,* and *Jesus* himself. Since these are individuals rather than groups, it is appropriate to ask what contemporary individuals are like these people. Since we are most likely preaching in a church to Christian people, our first approach will be to look for analogies between the characters in the text and ourselves as individual Christians. Once again we will be searching both for likeness and unlikeness. The procedure will be the same as we applied to groups in a text.

The Forgiven Woman. The first possibility is that we Christians are like the forgiven woman. She is in the first place a sinner. The tradition has identified her sin as prostitution, but we ought not to go beyond what the text itself says, which is simply that she is a sinner. This is not quite the thing we moderns like to say about people, but in the story there can be no doubt that she is a sinner. Simon the Pharisee knows this about her; such people always know. Jesus knows it about her also. Why else would he forgive her? She also knows it herself; it is because she knows she is a sinner that she is so extravagant in her gratitude when she experiences forgiveness. In the face of this unanimity in the story, our tendency to supply alternative explanations for ourselves, explanations that leave out sin, simply will not do.

Like her, we are sinners, as we may confess regularly in church: "We have done those things we ought not to have done, and have left undone those things we ought to have done, and there is no health in us."

The most important thing about the woman in the story is not, however, that she is simply a sinner, but that she is a *forgiven* sinner. This is shown by Jesus' own words, "Her sins though many are forgiven!" and by the overwhelming joy she shows in the face of that forgiveness. Her love and gratitude are the story's best witness to the reality of that forgiveness. We Christians also are forgiven sinners: "It is a saying worthy of complete acceptance that Christ Jesus came into the world to save sinners. In the name of Jesus Christ, I declare unto you that your sins are forgiven." Some such words are said to us every Sunday—or, if we do not belong to a church that makes use of a formal declaration of pardon, surely we sing "Amazing Grace" or one of a thousand other hymns that speak of the forgiveness that has come to a "wretch like me."

There is, of course, at least a small difference between the woman and ourselves. She really *knew* she was a forgiven sinner and reacted accordingly. She gave what she had, her tears, her hair, her perfume, her love, and simply did not stop giving. We, on the other hand, say the words, but the question remains how deeply many of us feel the genuine reality of either our sin or our forgiveness. Perhaps it would be different if we, like the woman, were objects of public scorn from people like Simon for our sin, but this is hardly the case for most of us. Those few people whom I have met who have experienced both the scorn and the forgiveness tend to share also the exuberance of the gratitude. Is this true for the rest of us?

Simon the Pharisee. Perhaps many of us in the church are more similar to Simon the Pharisee. He is, of course, painted rather negatively in the story; the storyteller means for us to dislike this man. It is often the negative characters who are most interesting, however. There are a few obvious resemblances to us church folk in Simon. He is religious, as are we. He is also righteous and respectable and quite ready to look down a morally superior nose at a "sinner." Very few churchgoers would be surprised to hear that some of us good church people can be all those nasty things. This is a staple insight of an inordinate number of sermons. (We preachers spend a great deal of time lambasting our listeners for self-righteousness. Indeed, we warn them so often against self-righteousness that some are afraid of any kind of righteousness at all!)

The most surprising thing about Simon is not that he is *righteous* but that he is *right*. Jesus tells Simon and us that quite clearly. "And Jesus said to him, 'You have judged rightly'" (v. 43). Simon is right not just about the interpretation of Jesus' little parable of the two forgiven debtors. He is right in virtually all his judgments. In fact, Simon is right about virtually every-thing in the story. This story is an example of a very clever storytelling technique in which those hostile to the faith speak the key testimony to the true nature of events. "It is expedient . . . that one man should die for the people," says Caiaphas, the high priest (John 11:50, KJV). "These people who have been turning the world upside down have come here also, . . . saying that there is another king named Jesus," say the Thessalonian per-secutors of Paul and his companions (Acts 17:6–7). They are, of course, quite right in their estimate of Paul and his fellow preachers. In a similar fashion, Simon's right judgments are the key to understanding this story. When Jesus allows the sinful woman to approach him, Simon says to him-self, "If this man were a prophet, he would have known who and what kind of woman . . . is touching him—that she is a sinner" (Luke 7:39). The as-sumption here is that a prophet is given by God the capacity to look into a situation or into human hearts and see what is truly there. Prophecy is more insight than foresight in this respect. Simon is quite right in this judgment also, but notice the result. By Simon's own standards Jesus is indeed a prophet, a prophet twice over. He does know what sort of woman the vis-itor is. If he did not know she was a sinner, why would he pronounce her forgiveness? Moreover, he can look into another heart and see what is there—the pride and the self-righteousness and above all the lack of love. It is his insight into Simon's own thoughts and words that bear clear testi-mony to Jesus' role. Jesus is by Simon's own correct standards a prophet, twice over.

I believe that we church people are often right in our standards and our judgments too. We're right about so many things. But being right is not good enough . . . if there is no love. And that is the trouble with Simon: true, he has never experienced very much in the way of sin; his debts may be small; still, he is not capable of very much love, and in Jesus' eyes that is the greatest wrongness of all. When we look in the mirror, do we see Simon?

While we are like Simon, nevertheless we need not identify with Simon exactly. We do not need to stay the same as Simon. There remains for us another possibility.

Jesus. There remains the third character in the story, Jesus. If Simon was righteous but not loving, and the woman was loving but not yet righteous, Jesus shows us what it is to be both righteous and loving. We are, of course, very different from Jesus. It is more than a little discomforting to notice that Jesus actually agrees with Simon about the woman; like Simon he knows that she is a sinner. The difference between the two lies not in the diagnosis, but in the treatment. Faced with a sinner, Simon offers only scorn. Faced with a sinner, Jesus gives forgiveness and love.

Many of us, even many of us church people, in the late twentieth century have grave difficulty with the concept of sin. We prefer other, seemingly less crude explanations of human behavior. Sin and forgiveness are realities of our liturgies, but not of our lives. Imagine for a minute that we are faced at this moment with the woman, and that she has not yet known forgiveness. It seems to me very likely that many of us would be tempted to deal with her not according to the categories of the Bible or of our liturgies, but according to the categories of our society. Faced with such a woman, we would be tempted to offer not forgiveness, but an explanation or even an excuse for her lot. If she then understood the psychological or sociological jargon in which we would very likely offer our explanation, she would go away . . . puzzled.

Explanations, whether psychological, sociological, or otherwise, can be genuinely helpful when dealing with troubled people. However, we in the church ought not abandon all but automatically the fundamental categories with which people of our faith have understood humanity in favor of such alternatives. It remains open to question whether understanding an explanation of our particular condition actually helps to heal the condition. If we were to offer an explanation rather than forgiveness, the woman would probably not cover our feet with her tears. Many a pastor and many a Christian, on the other hand, can bear witness to the healing power of forgiveness. I have never had anyone kiss my feet, but I once had an elderly woman, bedridden and lonely, kiss my hands. It happened when I acted as a minister and brought to her, as the church's servants have done for two millennia, the sacrament of forgiveness and love and acceptance.

Many of us might even be tempted merely to offer the easy word: "Hey, it doesn't matter." But the woman and those like her know better; they know that it, whatever *it* might be, does matter. She also knows that a refusal to take her sin seriously may well mask a refusal to take her seriously. "Hey, it doesn't matter" may simply be a comforting and socially acceptable way of saying, "Hey, *you* don't matter!" If we genuinely care about people, what they do and are *does* matter to us. How much of the tolerance in which many of us take pride is in fact nothing more than indifference? It is far easier to tolerate when we simply don't care about the other.

Hurting people in our world most certainly don't need our indifference, even if it wears the socially acceptable mask of tolerance.[8] Many do not even need or want our explanations for their condition; others can often do that better, in any case. They need not an explanation, but a word of forgiveness. If we in the church do not offer that forgiveness in Christ's name, who will? I heard recently from a former student who told me of visiting a dying woman who had been baptized but then lived a life totally apart from the church and, more important, from Christ. Because of the nature of her life she felt terribly ill prepared to meet her Creator. The minister sought to ease her fear: "Remember the story of the prodigal son," he told her. The woman had never heard or had completely forgotten that parable. What an experience it was, said the minister, to tell such a story as if for the first time to a person who desperately needed the forgiveness the Father offers. What a reaction there was when the woman heard, for the first time, the word of forgiveness! The old story was indeed Good News for the dying woman, the very news she needed.

> Jesus stands in any biblical text as another possibility for us.

Perhaps this is the way of Christ in the world: neither to minimize the sin nor to scorn the sinner. It would be terribly easy either to slip back into Simon's way of contempt or to accommodate to our culture of indifference. We know very well that in so many ways we are not like Christ, but he remains for us a possibility. Surely to grow up into the measure of Jesus Christ is the high goal of Christian life. Indeed, we should, perhaps, speak of something stronger than a possibility. "You have died and your life is hid in Christ," says the apostle Paul. What we truly are as Christians is what we are *in Christ*. Christian life consists of learning to be what we already are. The homiletical difficulty here is not in taking proper account of the difference between ourselves and Jesus, but in proclaiming convincingly the possibility and reality of our Christlikeness. The point is not that we *must* be like him but that, through the mercy of God, we *can* be like him.

Once again, when we have done this work we are not far from the sermon itself. Much of the material just written can be and indeed has been incorporated into a sermon on this rich and complex passage. It seems important here, however, to add another methodological observation that would not fit into a sermon on Luke 7:36–50. We may speak of Jesus even where Jesus is neither a character in the story nor the subject of discussion in the text. The context of any particular text is the canon as a whole, of which the life, death, and resurrection of Jesus Christ are the center for Christians. Moreover, we do not come to any text in that canon alone; we come as those who are *in*

Jesus Christ. Our point of contact with the text, our encounter with the word spoken there, is through him. Jesus stands in any biblical text as another possibility for us. So, for example, the sermon on Psalm 137 cannot be complete until it revisits the hatred in ourselves in company with Jesus Christ.

3. Decide if the text was a confirmation or a challenge to its first hearers. Determine whether the sermon should be a confirmation or a challenge to its hearers.

The question could be put this way: *Was the text good news or bad news for the first hearers, or both?*

It must be said immediately that the usual scriptural answer to this question must be "good news." The Bible as a whole is good news; it is a confirmation of God's undeserved love for all people. The story of Jesus is told, after all, in four "Gospels," a corruption of the Anglo-Saxon word for good news. Gospel itself is a literal translation of the Greek *euangelion,* which means "good news." The early Christian preacher of whom we know the most, the apostle Paul, wrote in 1 Corinthians 1:17: "For Christ did not send me to baptize but to proclaim the gospel." His primary task, he believed, was to tell "good news." One can reasonably expect that the individual texts of such a book will be primarily good news.

> The Bible as a whole is good news: it is a confirmation of God's undeserved love for all people.

This is far from the case with our sermons, however. When a teenager says, "Don't preach at me!" she doesn't mean, "Don't tell me good news!" She means, "Don't tell me what to do!" The boy who says, "I don't need a sermon!" really means, "Don't tell me what *not* to do." Somehow or other, we preachers have gained for ourselves the reputation of telling other people what and what not to do. Take out the phrase "somehow or other"! Anybody who listens to sermons knows exactly why people think that way about us and our sermons.

I was a high school classmate of my future brother-in-law, David. Shortly after my appointment to my present position, a third classmate was staying with David at the family summer cottage and asked after me. David said that I was now teaching "homiletics." "What's homiletics?" the friend replied. Somewhat puzzled, David looked up the word in a little dictionary we keep for Scrabble games. The word did not appear in the dictionary, but under the word "homily" there appeared the definition "a tedious moralizing discourse"[9]! I refuse to be defined as a person who teaches students how to deliver "tedious moralizing discourses"! A little attention to this question may be one means of saving us from delivering such "tedious moralizing discourses."

> Sermons are often not good news; they may be "tedious moralizing discourses."

It could, in fact, be said that there is no "bad news" in the Bible. The only truly bad news would be if God gave up speaking to us altogether. Even a word of chastisement from a good and loving God is good news. It shows that God cares about our evil and wills to put a limit on that evil. Surely that is in a way good news, particularly for those who suffer from evil.

Moreover, the law in the Old Testament—and the ethical exhortation which is its equivalent in the New—is not bad news, though we often manage to make it sound as if it were. It is "Torah," a word that might best be rendered "instruction." I remember trying to put together a gas barbecue with two other ministers, both of them as "hand tool challenged" as I. (One of them was my father-in-law. Don't tell him I wrote this!) Our worst trouble was that we found no instructions in the box. Just when frustration had reached the point at which we were about to do violence to one another with the hand tools, my wife found, wedged underneath a cardboard flap, the instructions! What a gift! The instructions themselves were good news.[10] Torah, understood in this sense, is anything but bad news.

But texts do not always feel like good news. Sometimes they are painful discipline indeed. At other times they lay terrifying demands on us. We meet God not only as total acceptance, but as total demand. The God who created heaven and earth and who redeemed us at the cost of the blood of Jesus Christ is not satisfied with easy acceptance. The preacher who proclaims acceptance but not repentance and obedience is not declaring the Christian gospel. We dare not preach what Dietrich Bonhoeffer called "cheap grace." Our God is not bought off with a sacrifice that costs us little. God's grace is free, but it is costly beyond human knowing. It required the life of Jesus Christ; it requires our life in response.

It is clear, moreover, that some texts primarily announce the good news; they are a confirmation of God's goodness to us. Others spell out the consequences of that goodness; they are a challenge to us. Still others do both. Perhaps a text is good news for one sort of person but very bad news indeed for another. The homiletical point here is quite simple. A sermon growing from a good news text ought itself to be good news. It ought to announce the presence of God's gracious love in the world and in our lives rather than laying yet one more task on the listeners. If the text lays out the consequences of trust and obedience, the sermon ought to the same. If it threatens judgment, the sermon may, under certain circumstances, do the same. Identifying the function of our texts in this respect is a homiletically vital task.

Sometimes it is quite easy to tell whether a text is good news or bad news. There is, for example, the familiar verse Luke 2:10, "But the angel said to them, 'Do not be afraid; for see—I am bringing you good news of great joy for all the people.'"

> Some tests are clearly either good news or bad news

This is obviously good news. Equally obvious is Isaiah 5:20–25:

> Ah, you who call evil good
>   and good evil,
> who put darkness for light
>   and light for darkness,
> who put bitter for sweet
>   and sweet for bitter!
> Ah, you who are wise in your own eyes,
>   and shrewd in your own sight!
> Ah, you who are heroes in drinking wine
>   and valiant at mixing drink,
> who acquit the guilty for a bribe,
>   and deprive the innocent of their rights!
>
> Therefore, as the tongue of fire devours the stubble,
>   and as dry grass sinks down in the flame,
> so their root will become rotten,
>   and their blossom go up like dust;
> for they have rejected the instruction of the LORD of hosts,
>   and have despised the word of the Holy One of Israel.
>
> Therefore the anger of the LORD was kindled against his people,
>   and he stretched out his hand against them and struck them;
>   the mountains quaked,
> and their corpses were like refuse
>   in the streets.

> For all this his anger has not turned away,
> and his hand is stretched out still.

There is good news in this text, but it is very indirect good news. It surely must have felt like bad news indeed to those who listened to Isaiah preach. In almost all cases in which a text is bad news it is because it pronounces judgment on some person or, more likely, some group. The key word here is judgment. God's word both saves and judges, and it is dangerous to ignore in our preaching the latter function.

Often a text is both good news and bad news. An example is Mary's Magnificat, Luke 1:46–55:

> And Mary said,
> "My soul magnifies the Lord,
> and my spirit rejoices in God my Savior,
> for he has looked with favor on the lowliness of his servant. . . .
> For the Mighty One has done great things for me,
> and holy is his name.
> His mercy is for those who fear him
> from generation to generation. . . .
> He has brought down the powerful from their thrones,
> and lifted up the lowly;
> he has filled the hungry with good things,
> and sent the rich away empty."

Clearly this text is good news—for the poor, that is—but it is bad news for the rich. Many texts are like this, good news under certain circumstances, bad news under others. This realization prepares us to understand that a text may be good news under the circumstances in which it was spoken but bad news under the vastly different circumstances of our lives. So, for example, Mary's Magnificat may be good news indeed for landless peasants in Latin America but function rather differently for wealthy North Americans.

> Many texts are good
> news to some and bad
> news to others.

CONFIRMATION AND CHALLENGE

If we change the categories from good news/bad news back to confirmation/challenge, we still see mixed types. Exodus 20:1 is an example:

> Then God spoke all these words: I am the LORD your God, who brought you out of the land of Egypt, out of the house of slavery; you shall have no other gods before me. . . .

The passage begins with confirmation, the announcement by which God designates himself as the one who had delivered the people from Egypt. It then presents the people with a solemn challenge to live according to that reality. "You shall have no other gods, shall make no graven images, shall not do murder or steal or commit adultery, etc." This is a common pattern. The pattern of confirmation followed by challenge is also, for example, the fundamental pattern of Paul's epistles. In the letter to the Romans, Paul speaks of the magnificence of God's plan of redemption in the free offer of grace laid hold of by faith in Jesus Christ. He culminates his argument in the eleventh chapter of his epistle with a magnificent doxology to God. He then says, "I appeal to you therefore, brothers and sisters, by the mercies of God, to present your bodies as a living sacrifice, holy and acceptable to God, which is your spiritual worship" (Rom. 12:1).

The word of challenge to faithful living is made on the basis of the confirmation of God's love found in Jesus Christ. The demand is based on the announcement of the good news. The theological point is that the confirmation is primary; the challenge is secondary and dependent on the confirmation. This suggests that there is a theological problem, not just a communication problem, with preaching that is as a whole bad news and challenge. There is something not only boring, but also sub-Christian about tedious moralizing discourses!

GOOD-NEWS PREACHING, BAD-NEWS SERMONS

The Bible as a whole is good news; our preaching as a whole should likewise be good news. If, over a period of time, those who listen to us preach have not clearly heard the good news that God loves us, we have failed as preachers. Once again a survey of our preaching over a period of time would be useful. We might profitably look at six months' worth of sermons and check whether we have been primarily heralds of good news or purveyors of bad tidings.

> The Bible as a whole is good news; our preaching as a whole should likewise be good news.

Nevertheless, there is in the Bible bad news, and most certainly there are many challenges. The law and the prophets bear witness to a God who is mercy itself and makes covenant with a people; they also lay before us the duty of obedience. We may not practice injustice; we may not practice idolatry. These things are violations of the covenant, and there may be terrible consequences if we do not obey! The New Testament bears witness to a love for us so great that it took our Lord Jesus to a cross. But that same Jesus also says to us, "Pick up *your cross* and follow me!" That is beyond doubt a challenge, and one that we ignore at our peril. He also said on occasion, "Woe to you!" to Chorazin, to Capernaum, to the rich. That sounds very much like bad news, at least to some people. While preaching as a whole must be good news and a confirmation of God's love for humanity, some individual sermons may be a challenge and even bad news. The practical question remains: When and how may we preach such sermons?

> Individual sermons may sometimes largely be challenge or even bad news.

In the first place, it is appropriate to preach a sermon that is primarily challenge if the text itself is primarily challenge. Even in such cases the challenge usually rests on good news. Remember Paul's appeal in Romans 12:1 (italics added here): "I appeal to you *therefore*"! Behind that one word "therefore" is the whole of the good news as Paul preached it. In theological terms, there is always a therefore of good news behind every text of challenge. Look for the grace of God; it will always be there somewhere in or around even a text of challenge. We must preach that good news as the basis for the challenge.

We may appropriately preach challenge when the people to whom we speak are analogically similar to those to whom the challenge comes in the text. It is true that we share with the people of the biblical world a common humanity and a common situation

> We may preach sermons that are primarily challenge if:
> (1) the text is primarily challenge
> (2) we have searched for the grace that is the basis for the challenge
> (3) the people to whom we are preaching are analogically similar to the people to whom the challenge first came
> (4) we remember that the challenge itself is more gift than burden.

as those addressed by God. The challenges and warnings of the Bible do therefore apply in a general way to us all. Nevertheless the situation to which we speak may be so different from the situation to which the text speaks that we cannot apply the text in a direct and simple way to our own situation. A friend and colleague once laughingly admitted to me that he had preached on the basis of a text in First Corinthians a sermon that sternly warned his sedate and formal upper-class congregation against the dangers of "enthusiasm." After the sermon his wife asked only, "Do you really think this congregation is likely to suffer from too much enthusiasm?" Finally, when we preach sermons that are primarily challenge rather than confirmation we would do well to remember that the law of God is instruction; it is "for our lasting good" (Deut. 6:24). Obedience, in this understanding, is not in the first place the taking up of a burden, but the receiving of a gift.

PREACHING BAD NEWS

Actually, although many homileticians strongly urge the preacher to emphasize good news, they also recognize that there are texts and occasions on which it is appropriate and necessary to preach sermons that are primarily a challenge to the listeners. A more difficult problem concerns texts like Isaiah 5:20–25 that seem to be entirely bad news. May preachers of the good news appropriately preach bad news, and if so when and how? Can such hard words of condemnation rightly be addressed to the church of Jesus Christ?

I fear that the word of challenge and even the bad news of judgment may sometimes be God's word for me, for us. I read Jeremiah and hear of preachers who cry, "'Peace, peace,' when there is no peace" (Jer. 6.14). I hear the words of the angel of the church in Laodicea: "I know your works: you are neither cold nor hot. . . . So, because you are lukewarm, and neither cold nor hot, I am about to spit you out of my mouth" (Rev. 3:15–16). I cannot help but fear that I am sometimes not unlike those preachers who proclaim too easy a peace. I sometimes imagine that the church in which I live is sometimes only . . . lukewarm. I dare not say, "Never preach bad news."

Some of the criteria for preaching bad-news sermons are the same as those for preaching challenge sermons. Once again, the text itself must be clearly a "bad-news" text and those to whom we are preaching must be analogically similar to the people to whom the bad news first came.

It is also the case that even judgment is not meant for evil, but for good. This latter point requires development. Judgment functions to limit the extent and the effect of evil, particularly on the oppressed. "God arose to establish judgment, to save all the oppressed of the earth" (Ps. 76:9). Surely this is why the psalmists so frequently call on God to arise and to execute judgment on the evildoer. Evil has a terrible, destructive effect on people and on the earth as a whole. Sometimes the effects of evil all but stare us in the face. I was recently in the African nation of Cameroon.

While walking one day I came across a small boy, perhaps two or three years of age, who looked up at the very tall white stranger in front of him with lovely brown eyes. He smiled at me. I looked down at him and saw that his legs were bowed like the letter c—doubtless from rickets, a condition caused by a dietary deficiency. I had to work very hard to smile back at the boy, for I knew that the dietary deficiency, in turn, is caused by poverty, and the poverty, at least in part, from a world system from which I profit. If God should arise even now and pronounce judgment on a world system that allows such things to be, can I repine? Should I not rather pray, "Let God rise up! Let God's enemies be scattered!" as Psalm 68:1 does, even if I am found to be one of those enemies? We may rightly pray that judgment should be delayed, but only so that the evil-doers, among whom we may be numbered, may find time for repentance and amendment of life. We may not pray that judgment should be delayed indefinitely.

We even have this further comfort: that the chastisement of God is not only for those who are oppressed—it is also for our good. It is the discipline of a loving parent who wills for us good and who wishes to save us even through judgment. The present moment is therefore a *kairos,* God's own time of grace granted to us in which we may turn from evil.

The name Jeremiah can remind us of another vital point: the preacher ought not to *enjoy* preaching bad news. Jeremiah is sometimes called the weeping prophet; to speak the harsh word that God had given him caused him great pain. Likewise Jesus wept over Jerusalem, "If you, even you, had only recognized on this day the things that make for peace!" (Luke 19:42). We may only safely preach bad news if we do so with tears in our eyes. Too often we take on ourselves the title "prophetic" preachers when actually we are simply indulging in the unworthy pleasure of enumerating the sins of others, the sins of our congregations and of the system by which we live. We sometimes appear to revel in haranguing our listeners for their sins. If we allow ourselves to preach this way very often, we do not last in congregations—we drift out of the church or find ourselves a niche in the structures of the church whose complicity in evil we publicly deplore. At all times, preachers must identify in love with those to whom they preach. This is never more true than when we are called to speak a harsh word. We may never preach hard words without tears in our eyes.

It is also always true that the text must speak to the preacher before it can speak to the congregation. This is true for all words from scripture, but is never more true than with the word of judgment. Such a word must speak to the preacher before the preacher can speak it to the congregation. We preachers must always include ourselves in the judgment that the text speaks.

There are two very practical consequences to this point. First, a vital part of the preparation of any bad-news sermon must be an unusually strenuous period of prayer and self-examination, so that we may know rightly the extent of our own complicity in evil. Second, we may never use the word "you" alone when speaking of judgment, but only "you and I," "we," or even "I."

I trust, and trust is the right word, that God will not in the end speak to us only the bad news of judgment. The key word remains grace. It is pure grace that God should speak to us at all. It is grace that delays judgment. It is grace alone that can save us even through judgment. Even a thoroughgoing bad-news sermon ought to point beyond its bad-news text to the grace in which alone we may put our trust.

> We may preach sermons that are primarily bad news if:
> (1) the text is primarily bad news
> (2) the people to whom we are preaching are analogically similar to the people to whom the bad news first came
> (3) we include ourselves in the bad news
> (4) we do not lose sight, even in the midst of the bad news, of the grace by which alone we may live.

4. Determine what the text does. Determine whether the sermon can appropriately do the same.

At this point we may appropriately ask ourselves the following set of questions:

What does the text do?

How can the sermon appropriately do the same?

Can those who are in Christ do what the text does?

Any meaningful text has a function—in other words, it does something. Asking what a text does is very much the same as asking what is its form. If we have discovered the form of the text during our exegesis, we can easily state what the text does. To identify the form of a text prepares us to identify the text's function. The question of form is not, therefore, merely a matter of labeling. We do not simply state that the text in question is a hymn or a lament or an exhortation or one of the many other form-critical categories developed by biblical scholars. Rather, it is a question of what the text *does,* of what function it fulfills. So, for example, a hymn offers praise, in poetic form, for the goodness of God. A lament bewails the sorry state of the people or of the singer. An exhortation, or *paranesis,* urges the reader or the community to take some course of action. And so on. Very close to the question of function is the question of the intended rhetorical effect of the text on the reader/hearer. A slightly extended form of these questions might therefore be: *What does our text do to and with its hearers? How can the sermon do the same to and with its hearers?*

> If we have identified the form of the text in our exegesis, we should already be able to answer the question, "What does the text do?"

A sermon should be more than the extended presentation of a concept or theme. We ought also to consider as preachers what it is that we believe our sermon should do, what its objective should be. It may be that the sermon should do in its new setting what the text did in its own setting.[11] It may be the case, however, that it is theologically inappropriate for the sermon to do what the text does.

In older preaching, the typical pattern was to distill from the text a fundamental idea or concept, to carry this concept across the chasm of time between text and contemporary world, and to divide, explain, and apply it. The exegetical task was to discover a "thematic residue" and to pour that residue into the sermon.[12] Texts in this view are only "inert containers for theological concepts."[13] In this pattern, the form of the biblical text made very little difference. The sermon form was more or less set; it would be in any case a discourse developing, in a more or less coherent manner, a particular proposition. Such preaching is sometimes called "propositional-discursive." More often it is simply stereotyped as "three points and a poem." The stereotype is more than a little unfair; many marvelous and edifying sermons have been preached using this form. The form in itself is, I believe, flawed, but it does not deserve mockery.

The role of the biblical text in this mode of preaching was chiefly to provide the proposition. (Sometimes biblical texts only illustrated the proposition.) So, for example, one could preach very much the same sermon on Jesus' parable of the unexpected coming of the Lord, Luke 12:35–40, as on Paul's exhortation to wait watchfully for the day of the

Lord in 1 Thessalonians 5:1ff. The same proposition could certainly be derived from both passages. By contrast, in contemporary homiletics the form of the biblical text is of first significance. Very often, of course, the text did not even fulfill that role; the proposition grew from general experience, common sense, the cultural values of the community, or even the preacher's favorite hobbyhorse.

One may compare the older opinion concerning the relation of homiletical form and content to traditional views of the relation of body and soul. In some popular theology the body does not matter—it may be stripped away and the soul freed of its fleshly shackles to enter heaven's gate. Similarly, the text may be freed of its form and the immortal concept may soar liberated into the sermon. A more appropriate comparison for good preaching might be to the Christian doctrine of the resurrection of the body. Ideas always are embodied in a form; they do not float wraithlike between heaven and earth. The sermon is the new "resurrection" body for conceptual material in the text. The question is whether the new body ought to have a form similar to that of its first body.

It is not the case that homileticians who urge us to pay attention to the form of the biblical text are saying that the sermon ought to be cast in the identical form, that a sermon on a biblical poem should itself be a poem, a sermon on a lament, a lament, and so forth. That would quickly become terribly impractical. Should, for example, a sermon on a proverb be a pithy three-second-long statement? Despite the fact that some long-suffering church-

> It may be that the sermon should do in its new setting what the text did in its own setting.

goers might shout "Yes!" in answer to that question, I cannot believe that form should be so ultimately determinative. Rather, the point is that the sermon most often should say and do in the contemporary setting what the text said and did in its setting. Thomas Long urges, for example, that we ask ourselves the following key question: "How may the sermon, in a new setting, say and do what the text says and does in its setting?"[14]

Answering this question may help save us from delivering "tedious moralizing harangues." The function of many texts in the Bible is clearly *not* "to tell us what to do or not to do." In such cases, and they are many, the function of the sermon need not be to tell the listeners what to do. Attention to this question or to the set of questions listed above may also be especially helpful when something seems to be going wrong with the sermon preparation. This sense of wrongness may come from an attempt to force the sermon to do something the text doesn't do. Let me use myself as the negative example here. I wrote my Ph.D. dissertation on the hymns of Luke's infancy narrative—the Magnificat, Benedictus, and Nunc Dimittis.[15] These are hauntingly lovely psalms of praise, echoing the praise of the Old Testament people of God, which appear in the midst of Luke's Christmas story. I spent several years studying these hymns because I loved their beauty.

It eventually came time to preach on the first of these hymns, the Magnificat. From the text I took the proposition, a correct and exegetically defensible one, in my opinion, "God is on the side of the poor and the oppressed." The sermon fell flat. It seemed to me dry and lifeless, displaying none of the attractiveness that had drawn me to the poem in the first place. The people at the door were indifferent, polite at best. A while later I tried again. This time I derived from the text the proposition "We ought to be on the side of the poor and the oppressed." This time the indifference disappeared; I suppose that, at least, was a good thing. But the indifference was replaced by irritation, even by outright anger. Several self-serving explanations were possible. Perhaps a conservative church was simply unable to hear such a stern and prophetic word. That would let the preacher, me, off the hook! In fact, the congregation in question was largely made up of people to the left of me politically. Perhaps, as somebody said in response to my laments about the failure of the sermon, it is very difficult to preach from a passage that one knows so well. I didn't like that idea; surely one would not want to argue that the more thorough the exegesis, the worse the sermon. But whatever the reason, the hymn of praise had become in my sermon a "tedious moralizing discourse," and a politically correct one at that.

So the matter rested until I taught my first homiletics class. By then I had read some homiletical theory and knew that I ought to urge my students to pay attention not only to the form but also to the content of the biblical text. At that point, and only then, it occurred to me that I had caused my own problems by ignoring the very advice that I was now passing on to the students. Eventually I decided to preach again on the passage. The Magnificat, I now noted, is a psalm that offers exuberant praise to God. A sermon on this psalm might rightly praise God with exuberance and invite the congregation to share in that praise. If I were to summarize the psalm, I would now say, "Mary is so awed by the reversal of expectations that God has wrought that she bursts forth in praise to God." How could she help but sing?

I knew from my exegetical work that the Magnificat was a psalm of the early Christian church, which consisted of folk who were by no means high on the social scale. What Paul said of the church at Corinth was true of most early Christians: "Not many . . . wise, . . . not many . . . of noble birth." But they believed that the world had been "turned upside down" in the life, death, and resurrection of Jesus Christ, and all purely human expectations had been set aside. That is why they burst forth in songs of praise like the Magnificat. How could they help but sing?

It was appropriate now to look for analogies to Mary and to the early Christians and their experience of a world turned upside down. I found this in the experience of base communities of Latin America, groups of Christians who, in their poverty, hear, perhaps for the first time, that God is on their side. Nothing is as exciting as this notion; by comparison the *Communist Manifesto* is dull indeed. How could they help but sing?

I found something like that joy even in the experience of Christians in quite ordinary congregations in my own country. Nobody expects very much of such congregations; often the members of these churches cannot even get their own children to attend. Certainly the opinion molders of our society do not think highly of these bodies; they pay attention only when they want to write a story of the decline and imminent death of mainstream Christianity. But the people of the church actually encounter God in this place. Their worship, their fellowship with one another, actually gives them so profound a sense of the presence of God that even the inevitable frustrations and difficulties of a congregation's life cannot take away their underlying joy. So, how can they help but sing?

The progression of the sermon was:

Mary
the early Christians
Latin American Christians
the local church

Each experienced an amazing reversal of expectation; each saw or can see signs of God's presence and work in ordinary-appearing circumstances, and each responded or responds in praise.

This sermon, after I took account not only of concepts in the text but also of its form, was in the end satisfying. Few of our texts deliver tedious moralizing discourses; perhaps if we pay attention to what they actually do, we also will deliver fewer of the beasts.

There are times, however, when it would be a serious mistake for the preacher to do what the text does. Consider Psalm 137 again, as an example.

The first part of the psalm bewails and laments the lot of an exiled people in misery. Preachers in wealthy North American congregations can hardly do the same in their sermons. If we did, it would not be, "By the waters of Babylon — there we sat down and there we wept." It would be, in my geographical location, "By the waters of Lake Ontario, there we sat down and whined." To complain bitterly about our lot is, for most of us, simply not a very attractive option.

> There are times when it is not appropriate for the preacher to do what the text does.

Even worse is the end of the psalm. The psalmist expresses bitter hatred for the Babylonian enemies, "Happy shall they be who take your little ones and dash them against the rock!" Can a Christian minister say such things? Faced with difficult texts such as this, some preachers decide to preach "against the text."

Ronald Allen states the situation succinctly: "In some cases biblical texts articulate viewpoints that are not appropriate to the spirit of gospel, that are unintelligible, or (and) may lead to immoral behavior."[16] Psalm 137 is alarmingly intelligible, but it certainly meets points one and three of Allen's terrible trio. It breathes a spirit decidedly inappropriate to the spirit of the Gospel (I would prefer the capital letter). It also, if taken as a prescription, would lead to immoral behavior. Many consider it permissible to "preach against the text" in such circumstances.

I remain uncomfortable with the phrase "preaching against the text," however. The trouble is that one may decide what is "appropriate" or "immoral" according to one's own ideology. The ideology would judge the sufficiency of scripture rather than allowing scripture to judge the sufficiency of our ideology. I, for one, am too suspicious of prevailing ideologies to be happy with that procedure. The canon for judging the appropriateness of a text ought not be our own ideology but the center of scripture itself, namely, the revelation of God in Jesus Christ. This is an ancient interpretative principle — that the unclear should be judged by the clear and the peripheral by the central. Scripture has a clear center, the person of Jesus Christ. We as Christians are "in Christ" and should judge our relationship to particular texts (not precisely the texts themselves) from that vantage point. My own way of rephrasing Allen's criteria is to ask the question: *"Can those who are in Christ do what the text does?"* In this case, I remember the words of

> The criterion for judging the appropriateness of a text ought not to be our own ideology but the center of scripture itself, the revelation of God in Jesus Christ.

Christ from the cross: "Father, forgive them; for they do not know what they are doing," and I believe that the answer with respect to Psalm 137 must be "No." The sermon therefore cannot appropriately do what the text does. Whatever we do with this text, we cannot justify such hatred.

This last question functions as a check on the first two. In many cases it will be appropriate for the sermon to do in its new setting what the text did in its setting . . . but not always.

5. Share the movement of the text.
Is there a movement through the text
which the sermon can follow?

An important possibility for effective preaching is that the sermon may share the movement of the text. Various methods of literary criticism can help us discern that movement. Once the movement of the text is determined, the preacher may look for analogies not simply between characters in the text and persons or groups in the contemporary world, but between the processes laid bare in the literary analysis on the one hand and our lives on the other. Using this approach, one can speak powerfully of the varied ways God deals with humanity and the multitude of human interactions with God and other humans.

> It is not only the persons or groups but also the movements in the text that may be analogous to realities in our lives. Look for those movements!

In this chapter I intend to apply several variants of literary criticism to the interpretation of the well-known but ill-named parable "the prodigal son." If we had applied to this text the questions discussed earlier, we would already have identified three main characters — the father, the older son, and the younger "prodigal," or wasteful, son. We would have supposed that these figures are to some degree representative of God, the righteous, and forgiven sinners respectively. We would then have compared ourselves, probably meaning by "ourselves" members of the church, to at least the last two characters. The results would probably have been fruitful. It may be, however, that such identifications would produce a rather static and lifeless, even predictable sermon. It may be that it is not merely the case that we are like (or unlike) characters in the story, but that the movements and transformations experienced in the text are somehow similar to our own life experiences. What happens to and in the characters is perhaps similar to what happens to and in us. A sermon that takes account of these movements and transformations might be considerably richer than the first sort. Various forms of literary criticism, especially narrative criticism and rhetorical criticism, can help us get at these transformations or movements in the text.[17]

Almost all commentators note the careful construction of Luke 15 and consider it to be a literary unit.[18] It would be entirely possible to treat it exegetically as a unit and then to preach on the three "lost" parables of Luke 15 as a whole. In this case, however, I shall discuss only the last of the three parables. It is substantially different in nature from the lost sheep and the lost coin parables, which are almost exactly parallel one to the other.[19] It is a much longer and more developed narrative than the lost coin or the lost sheep. Like a number of Jesus' other parables, it is a "two peaked Parable,"[20] which presents to the listener/reader two very different types of persons and two possibilities of relationship with God. It would be possible and appropriate to preach either on what is common to the three parables or on the development that is distinctive to the last of the three. It is not, therefore, a violation of the artistic integrity of the chapter to confine my intention to the so-called "prodigal son."

Older commentators by no means ignored the fact that this parable is a narrative, but it is interesting for the purpose of contrast to my own treatment of the text briefly to note the kinds of concerns that occupy at least part of their attention. A selection of the more significant commentators shows the following: Did Jesus say the three parables on the same occasion? What were the laws of inheritance in the time of Jesus? Is the second half of the story original or, on the other hand, was it added by Luke or in the tradition? Was leaving home a sin? Had there been a *ketsatsah,* a ceremony of cutting the sinner off from Jewish society?[21] The questions are certainly interesting, particularly to the historian rather than to the preacher, but they are ignored in a literary-critical approach to the text.

Stephen D. Moore has written, "Narrative criticism is a story-preoccupied gospel criticism. Being preoccupied with story means, most of all, being preoccupied with plot and character." He defines plot as "a set of events linked by temporal succession and causality."[22] Character is related to plot: "Characters are defined in and through the plot, by what they do and by what they say. The plot in turn comes into view as characters act and interact."[23] It is time therefore to consider plot and character. Consider the movements of characters in the text:

1a. The younger son goes to a far country.
2a. The younger son draws near home.
3a. The father goes to meet the younger son and brings him home.

1b. The older son goes to the field.
2b. The older son draws near home.
3b. The father goes to meet the older son.

There is one element missing in the parallelism, a mention of the older son coming home. The reason for this apparent omission may be the key to understanding the text as a whole.

The movements may be diagrammed like this:

YOUNGER SON

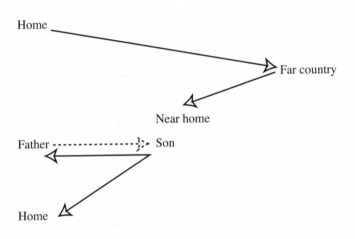

OLDER SON

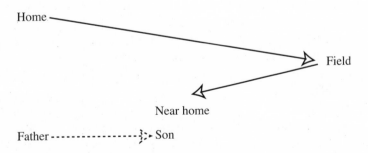

?

The question mark appears because we do not know whether the older son gets over his anger and returns home. The parable appears to be incomplete in that respect.

The remarkable thing about this parable is that these physical movements of the characters match transformations in the status of the characters. The younger boy begins the story as a son: "Then Jesus said, 'There was a man who had two sons. The younger of them said to his father, "Father, give me the share of the property that will belong to me." So he divided his property between them'" (vv. 11–12).

This young man travels to the far country, wastes his money (a fool and his money are soon parted!), and is forced to sell his services to a local farmer. There in the pigpen "he came to himself"—a very accurate translation of the telling Greek phrase.[24] It is important to note that his reflections concern his status and the disastrous change that has occurred in that status. His status is very different now; he is not worthy to be called a son. In fact, he recognizes that he has made himself something worse than one of his father's hired servants. One could ask who, like the son, could be worse off than a hired servant; the answer is "a slave." In effect, the transformation in status is from son to slave. The young man does not explicitly call himself a slave in the narrative, however. He does not say, "Here I am, no better than a slave!" The reason for this reticence will become clear when considering the story of the older brother. At any rate, the status of hired servant would be a marked improvement in his lot and worth the trouble of a long journey home (vv. 17–19). It is worthy of note that the young man can indeed take action to alter his status for the better. He cannot, however, restore that which has been lost; only the Father can grant sonship. To be a son (or a daughter) is to be in a situation of relationship, and a relationship depends not only on one's own intentions but on the grace of another. The young man then returns home hoping, as we have seen, to improve his status to that of hired servant. His father, however, sees him from a great distance, runs to him, and embraces him. He scarcely listens to the boy's carefully rehearsed speech, but calls for the robe, the ring, the sandals, and the fatted calf. These are all signs of a renewed status. The boy is a son again and, as in the previous two parables, there is great rejoicing.

It is time to turn with the narrative to the older son. This young man is certainly an unpleasant character, as the evangelist is at considerable pains to show. He omits any honorific in addressing his father (v. 29); he cuts himself off from his brother, calling him "this son of yours"! He knows how his brother has lost his money—with prostitutes, a detail which the first half of the story pointedly does not supply (v. 30). Perhaps the key thing, however, is that the older son too is away from home. But once again this is more than physical circumstance; the distance reflects the status. This young man has also been a son. In fact, as the older son he holds the higher status.[25] But here too is tragedy. "Listen! For all these years I have been working like a slave for you," he says to his father (v. 29). Perhaps a better translation would be "all these years I have slaved for you" (the key word is a verb in the Greek). Luke Timothy Johnson's translation emphasizes the present reality of the slavery—"Look, I am slaving for you."[26] What has been implicit with the younger son is explicit with the older. He has traveled nowhere; his far country is of his own making. The poor boy has made himself a slave in his own father's house! The transformation is parallel to that of his younger brother, and without the fun. There is tragedy here. The older son has also lost his identity, and at this point in the story we do not know precisely who he is.

There is also love. The father has left the house to seek this son too: and claims this son too: "Son, you are always with me, and all that is mine is yours." We do not know if the older brother hears the father's appeal, comes out of his snit, and comes into the party.[27]

A diagram of all this will look familiar (see next page).

The two halves of the parable are parallel in their movement and structure, but the second half remains incomplete. What all this suggests is that the story was written for the sake of the older son. It is aimed not so much at younger sons or daughters who already have come home, but to the older sons and daughters who still need to come home and may not even know that they need to come. That the relation of the father and the older son is the key one in the chapter is shown by the structure of the narrative and the position of the dialogue with the older son at the climax of that narrative.

It is also shown by the fact that this part of the story forms an inclusion with the beginning of the chapter. Luke tells us quite baldly who is the "target" of these stories. "Now all the tax collectors and sinners were coming near to listen to him. And the Pharisees and the scribes were grumbling and saying, 'This fellow welcomes sinners and eats with them.' So he told them this parable" (Luke: 15:1–3).

Perhaps it is for this reason that the text makes the clear statement about enslavement with respect to the older son, not the younger. It must be made clear that the real problem of slavery is not primarily that of the forgiven sinner, but that of the unrepentant righteous.

At this point it is necessary to leave this brief exercise in narrative criticism behind. We need to ask the rhetorical-critical question, "What was Luke trying to do with respect to his audience?" Many commentators have noted a number of the considerations brought forward in this chapter and assume that there is here a polemic against the Pharisees. So, for example,

YOUNGER SON

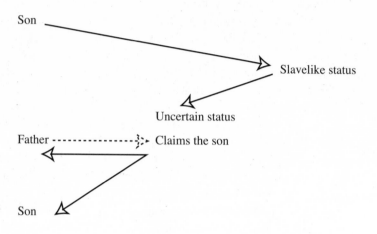

OLDER SON

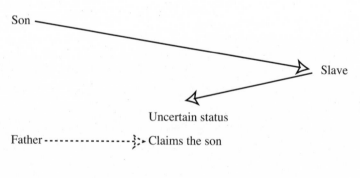

?

we read, "Yes, Luke 15 is about the grace of God, but it also serves an important function as a critique of the errant attitude of the Pharisees and their failed responsibility for seeking the lost."[28] One must ask why Luke would do this. Is Pharisaism a living option for "Theophilus" or for the members of his church? Was Luke's church populated by Jewish Christians tempted to return to their ancestral ways or at least threatened by Judaism in some way? The answer to these questions is probably "No."

More significant, if it had really been Luke's purpose to draw as negative a picture of the Pharisees as possible, he ought not to have left the end of the parable "open." He could easily have had the older son reject the appeal of the father. Moreover, the father warmly expresses his love for the older son and announces that all that he has belongs to the son, unconditionally. It is not even dependent on coming into the party. Perhaps, one could argue, all this love is described with a view to magnifying the culpability of the older brother when he rejects the invitation, but, once again, the older brother does not in fact reject the invitation. The author of this parable is, beyond argument, an extraordinarily skillful storyteller. Such an artist would not be guilty of so obvious a failure if it had been his intention merely to attack the elder brother/Pharisees.[29] An "open" conclusion must be directed to those whose situation is "open," that is to say, those who yet have the possibility of coming into the party.

I can only suggest here what ought to be argued, namely, that Luke is primarily directing his gospel not against Jews but to a Christian church. Luke is not writing his gospel for Palestinian Jews near the beginning of the first century, but for people like the most excellent Theophilus. His audience and church are not primarily Jewish, but Gentile. They live somewhere in the Roman Empire toward the end of the first century. They probably know tax collectors and sinners (who doesn't!), but they probably have never met a Pharisee. Luke is doing more than giving them a certain amount of historical information about the way things were a half century earlier in Palestine; he is addressing them in their situation. He is at least as much a preacher as a historian. The older brother is therefore not simply a representative of long-dead Pharisees and the scribes—he pictures a living possibility for the church. He represents a possibility that Christians might embody. Christians in Luke's church, tempted to self-righteousness, unwilling to welcome the sinner, ought to see themselves in this figure.

Luke is, at this point and, I believe, at many others in the Gospel, using the technique of analogy. It is true that he wanted his readers to see the obvious analogy between the older brother and the scribes and Pharisees. He wanted them also, I believe, to see an analogy between themselves and the older brother.

Did it work? We have no information on the subject, but perhaps we can speak of our own churches. In my experience most

> Luke may have made use of analogy as he wrote the Gospel.

people in church feel a measure of sympathy for him—a sure sign that listeners are themselves thinking analogically. They recognize the older son in the mirror. It would not be surprising if this were true also in Luke's church. In short, Luke may have been an analogical preacher!

An analogical sermon on a narrative such as this parable might appropriately take the form of an amplified retelling of the biblical narrative. In the course of the retelling it would be possible and homiletically effective to link ourselves analogically with the various characters in the story.

First, it should be noted that the analogical link is not merely to the characters in the story ("We are the prodigal"/"We are the older son"), but to the movement of the story. It is a link to that interaction of plot and character that makes up the story. That movement also gives shape and coherence to the sermon as a whole. Such a sermon would be expository, following not the artificial and secondary divisions we call verses, but the movement that is there in the story itself.

Of the characters in the story, the most important is the father; he alone is a major character in both episodes of the parable. It is also reasonably clear that the father, while not identified as God, portrays for us some of God's nature and for that reason also is the key theological character in the story. The parable might, in fact, be better called "The Waiting Father."[30]

A real danger of the analogical approach to the text is that it can easily become almost exclusively anthropocentric. By looking for analogies between characters or groups in the text and our own situation we may direct our thoughts chiefly to our own situation rather than to God's activity in the text or in the world. It is also important therefore to seek analogies between what God is shown to be doing in the text and what God is or may be doing in our world. With that note in mind, we may safely turn to the two sons.

The analogies between the situation of many in our society and the younger son suggest themselves powerfully. In the story the young man moves from the status of son to that of something very much like a slave. This transformation in status reflects a loss of freedom, that state precious to most humans.[31] How many children of God seek freedom and misuse that gift from God? Freedom misused, freedom abused, is freedom lost. How many children of God lose that freedom and make themselves slaves? There are pigpens in every city and town where children of God starve themselves. Some of the pigpens are obvious—addiction and alcohol, gambling and destructive sexual practices—but others are less obvious. Many a child of God is a self-sold slave in a million-dollar home. Even a mansion can be a far country if the child of God who lives there is a slave. But there is great good news here: any child of God will be welcomed home, not grudgingly but with rejoicing. God rejoices when the lost are found.

The story does not end here, however; neither can the sermon. We must return to the older son precisely because our narrative analysis has shown him to be the one addressed at the climax of the story and because so many in our churches recognize themselves in him. The nature of this analogy, too, is worthy of exploration. Do we in the church not often cut ourselves off from the rest of humanity: "This daughter, this son of yours!" We too, like the older son, are ready to believe the worst about our sisters and brothers, even in the absence of evidence. The figure in the mirror is not particularly likable. But the greatest tragedy is that we have made ourselves slaves in our own family home. We have gone to a far country without leaving home, and a gray, dim, dismal place it is indeed. We have not lived as much-loved children of a loving God, but as slaves. We have been bound primarily to rules and regulations, rather than to a relationship. We may not even be able to celebrate the love of God. But the main thing about us is this: we are still loved. God loves us every bit as much as the spectacular sinner, and indeed comes to us in our far country and invites us, begs us, to come into the party.

That is why the story is left incomplete in Luke 15—so that we might tell the end of the story, so that we might leave behind our slavery, our self-righteousness, our pride, and come into the party.[32]

PREACHING BEYOND THE PERICOPE

If we are intending to allow the movement of biblical texts to help shape our sermons, it is entirely possible that we shall have to leave behind the boundaries of the pericope. That is to say we may not, from time to time, preach only on a pericope, a specific delimited biblical text, but on the relationship among texts or the development between texts. It is possible that it is not only in the texts themselves but in their relationship to one another that we shall discover the movements and transformations that will enliven our preaching.

> Looking for movements and transformations may take us beyond the boundaries of individual texts, or pericopes.

One of the first duties of the preacher who cares at all for the biblical text is to answer the question "How much Bible will I use?" This is connected to, but not wholly determined by, the question "How much am I going to read aloud in church?" (The latter question is determined for many of us by the lectionary.) Frequently, there is within the reading what might be called an "effective text" with which the preacher will actually work and from which the sermon will grow. So, for example, the preacher may read aloud Mark 2:23–28, the pericope of the disciples in the grainfield on the sabbath, but preach only from verse 27, "The sabbath was made for humankind, and not humankind for the sabbath." At times the reading and the effective text are more or less the same. Occasionally the preacher will deal with an effective text wider than that actually read aloud. Determining the limits of the "effective text" of our sermon is a primary homiletical task that will greatly influence all the other choices the preacher will subsequently make.

We do not make this primary choice in a vacuum. There are trends both in homiletics and in biblical studies that have made certain choices more probable than others. At present, in homiletics "the pericope rules." Biblical scholars are no longer fixated on pericopes, however, but also consider the meaning of larger units of thought within books. This has not yet changed the reality that in preaching the pericope still reigns supreme.[33] Most homiletical texts that devote a section to exegetical concerns begin, as a result, with a demand that the preacher first determine the boundaries of the text. This present work is no exception.

One should also not underestimate the impact of the popularity of the Common Lectionary, which is also pericope-based. It is true that the choice of boundaries of the texts suggested by the lectionary authorities in its original version was sometimes puzzling, to say the least,[34] but there cannot be any doubt that those authorities did try to divide the text into a series of pericopes that correspond with units of thought in the biblical texts. The system also tried, however, to set those pericopes into a canonical context. In fact, one of the great virtues of lectionary-based preaching is that the preacher can if, she wishes, pay attention to that context.

But this may not be enough. It is true that there will always be a need for sound pericope-based preaching. The preacher is limited by time; he can take up only so much Bible in the typical hour-long service. The pericope is a reasonable and responsible unit to deal with in this limited time.

> Sometimes an entire book is the appropriate text for preaching.

But more remains to be said. I believe there is room for preaching that breaks the bond of the pericope, that faithfully deals with the text in its wider context.

Take for example, the book of Jonah. Is it genuinely responsible to deal with any one part of this text in isolation from the whole? Jonah 2:2–9, for example, is a unit of thought, a hymn, but on its own has little significance. This and other individual parts make very little sense except in the context of the book as a whole. A fine sermon on Jonah is presented in William Carl's

Preaching Christian Doctrine.[35] There, Carl deals not with a particular text in Jonah but with the book as a whole. Similarly, it is extraordinarily difficult to preach on the book of Job without dealing with the entire story. Calvin in his first sermon on Job wrote, "In order to profit well from what is contained in the present book, we must first of all understand the sum of it."[36] The meaning of the story is not found in any particular subunit, but in the development that takes place in Jonah, book and prophet, as a whole. All this we recognize without any great difficulty. The most reasonable unit of meaning in such cases is obviously the entire book.

Sometimes the most reasonable unit of meaning is a cycle within a book. How could one preach from Genesis 50:20, "Even though you intended to do harm to me, God intended it for good," as Joseph says to his brothers, without recounting most of the Joseph cycle? That verse is the climax not just of a pericope, but of the Joseph story as a whole. One could well preach on Elijah at Horeb where he complains, "I alone am left, and they are seeking my life, to take it away" (1 Kings 19:10, 14) or on the "sound of sheer silence" (v. 12) that signals the presence of God. But do these verses have meaning apart from the Elijah cycle? Sometimes the most reasonable unit of meaning is greater than the pericope. Where this is the case, our "effective text" should be greater than the pericope.

> Sometimes the most reasonable unit of meaning is a cycle within a book.

But what about the Gospels? Here the pericope is often identical with a form-critical unit. But even here, is it not the case that the position of a pericope is a large part of its meaning? Students at Knox College, where I teach, remember well their longtime professor of Old Testament language and literature, Stanley Walters. Professor Walters's most-remembered saying is "Position is hermeneutic." No pericope, with the arguable exception of the pericope *adulterae,* John 8:1–11, stands alone. What a text means is at least heavily influenced and perhaps determined by its position in the text.

If such is the case, responsible preaching from time to time is well advised to take up such questions. In these cases the preacher addresses not merely the meaning of a particular text, but its interrelationship with those around it. Preaching beyond the pericope is not only permissible, but from time to time required. Put briefly, it is vital to preach on the forest as well as on the trees.

Take, for example, the story of the paralytic let down through the roof, Mark 2:1–12 and parallels. It is magnificent preaching material. Form-critically it is an altered "tale" or miracle story. The classic elements of such a pericope are present: setting, problem, response, proof. The additions to the form are also fascinating. We note the emphasis on the faith of the friends, not of the paralytic—a surprise to many students. The New Testament never offers a definition of faith, but faith can be recognized when seen. "When Jesus saw their faith. . . ." Is there a better picture of the determination and audacity of faith than the friends up on the roof with shovel and crowbar, preparing to let down their friend before Jesus? We hear the controversy between Jesus and the experts in the law, not just locals but from Jerusalem, the heart of Judaism, according to Luke. Both Luke and Mark cleverly make these experts bear witness to the uniqueness of Christ by saying the truly vital thing in the pericope: "Only God can forgive sins!" Then, of course, Jesus forces them, and the reader, to face the central question of just who he is by healing the man as a proof of his authority to forgive sins. There would be no lack of material for several sermons by staying within the pericope itself.

But consider also its position in the Gospels. In Mark and Luke the story initiates a series of pericopes, all of which end in conflict with the religious authorities.

1. Jesus heals a paralytic: Trouble over the forgiveness of sins.
2. The call of Levi: Jesus associates with sinners.
3. The question about fasting: Jesus does not enforce this religious duty on his disciples.
4. The grainfields on the sabbath: Jesus does not enforce sabbath regulations.
5. Jesus heals on the sabbath.

At this point (Mark 3:6; Luke 6:11), as the culmination not simply of the last pericope in the series but of the series itself, the authorities begin to plan how they might harm Jesus. The shadow of the cross falls across the Gospel at this early point, well before the "first prediction" of the Passion. Note that it is Jesus at his most characteristic who offends: he heals, he forgives, he liberates from a burdensome interpretation of the law. It is this which sets him on the path to Golgotha. It is not a misunderstood Jesus, but one who is seen for what he is, who is rejected and in the end crucified.

All this cannot be seen or heard clearly if the preacher is confined to one pericope at a time. The lectionary does cover these texts in canonical order. But it is expecting too much of our people to be present for and remember clearly the pattern that extends over five pericopes. Surely, the pattern itself is worth preaching and this can be done only if the preacher extends the effective text beyond the pericope.

Consider also the story of Mary and Martha and Jesus in Luke 10:38–42. The interpretative tradition seems terribly uncomfortable with this little pericope and its apparent downgrading of service in favor of contemplation. To solve this problem, many commentators seek to find a balance between Mary and Martha that is, to be frank, not there in the text. This is probably bad exegesis, but it may rest on a sound theological instinct. It is, indeed, contrary to the witness of scripture as a whole totally to subordinate doing to listening.

A student at Knox College, Hugh Donnelly, wrestled in his first-year sermon with just this problem. He noted that earlier in the chapter a lawyer has asked Jesus what should be considered the greatest commandment (Luke 10:25). The answer is clear: "Love God with all that you are and your neighbor as yourself." The second part of this commandment, concerning the love of neighbor, is then explained in the story of the good Samaritan. The first part of the commandment, concerning the love of God, is then exemplified in Mary.[37] This creates a neat chiasmus, ABBA, where A is the love of God and B is the love of neighbor. Now, as is appropriate, Hugh could speak of a balance between hearing and doing in the persons not of Mary and Martha but of Mary and the Samaritan. Older interpreters seeking this balance did violence to the pericope. Hugh did justice to the wider structure.[38]

> Sometimes it is appropriate to preach on the relationship between neighboring texts rather than on the texts themselves.

Sometimes to ignore these matters is, in fact, to do violence to our texts. Justo and Catherine Gonzalez note that the excision from Matthew 2 by the lectionary of the tale of the slaughter of the innocents as an effective text distorts the meaning of the text in favor of the rich and wise.[39] By contrast Fred Craddock, in his powerful sermon "The Hard Side of Epiphany," draws the pain and strength that make the sermon what it is from the juxtaposition of the visit of the Magi and the slaughter of the babies of Bethlehem.[40]

Finally, it should be stated that the ultimate unit of meaning for biblical preaching is the canon of scripture itself. This "vast, loosely-organized, non-fiction novel" is in the end the most reasonable unit of meaning for us. In a society and church that no longer know the story, surely it is right and

proper to use the canon of scripture itself as our effective text. From time
to time it may be appropriate to provide in a single sermon the outline of that story as a whole.[41]

> The story of the Bible as a whole can even become the text for our preaching.

Several conclusions suggest themselves as a result of all this:

a. The pericope can be and doubtless will remain the primary effective text in biblically responsible preaching. The pericope is the basic building block in the structure of many books of the Bible, most notably the Gospels. To use a different metaphor, the pericope is the fundamental episode in the narrative that is the Bible as a whole. Preaching is necessarily episodic, "Same time next week!" and so it makes sense primarily to follow the Bible's own episodes. Pericopes are manageable units of thought, which adapt themselves well to the preaching task; they have also been the primary focus of a considerable proportion of the biblical interpretation that can provide rich resources for the preaching task.

b. Preaching on pericopes should also be supplemented with homiletical consideration of wider units of thought. It is entirely appropriate for the effective text to be a book or a cycle within the book. Perhaps the key question to ask is, "Does the individual text make sense apart from a recounting of the wider unit of thought?"

c. Contemporary biblical studies are not confined to the pericope but consider carefully units wider than the pericope. Homiletics can appropriately follow this lead. Where such consideration is particularly enlightening, the preacher often has the responsibility of extending the text beyond the pericope. Where these studies display a coherent movement or transformation between texts, it is particularly appropriate to preach from the whole movement rather than simply from one pericope.

d. If not at the beginning of a series of sermons on a particular book, at some point in our preaching it is our task to expose our congregations to the book as a whole and to its place within the biblical witness as a whole. Often it will also be possible to preach with power not on texts in themselves but on the juxtaposition of texts or on the way texts fit into patterns within a book. Following the lectionary by no means relieves us of this responsibility. If we do not provide some introduction to the canonical framework of the lectionary texts, our people will inevitably interpret them in light of the artificial framework provided by the lectionary itself. If anything, preaching from the lectionary requires an increased attention to biblical context as a counterbalance to this tendency.

e. Sometimes it may be necessary to use as our effective text the scriptural story as a whole. We can preach not only on the developments and transformations within pericopes and between pericopes but on the transformation that occurs in the scripture as a whole. If the pericope is the tree, the Bible is the forest. Much preaching will speak, rightly, of the individual tree. In the past some preaching has focused almost exclusively on the twigs on the tree's outermost branch. But surely sometimes the preaching of the church will lift its eyes from the trees and recognize that we are standing in a forest.

6. Testify to the work of God.
What is God doing in the text?
Is God doing anything similar in our world?

A ditch lies somewhere very near our feet, and I am about to lead you into it as, inadvertently in my blindness, I led some of my early classes. After a while I noticed with some dismay that my students, my *good* students in particular, were composing careful, intelligent sermons that made wise observations about humanity but rarely spoke of God. I wondered why this was the case until I realized that they were doing exactly what I had taught them to do. They were drawing analogies between persons and groups in the world of the text and persons and groups in our world, and nothing more. The trouble with analogical preaching that begins with human figures and groups in or behind the text is that it may likewise end there, with humanity. Such preaching may become anthropocentric rather than theocentric or Christocentric. To paraphrase Karl Barth, we cannot preach about God by talking about humanity in a loud voice. The chief character in the Bible is always God, and it is God's word that we desire to speak in our sermons. To make clever comparisons between what humans did or experienced several thousand years ago and what humans do and experience now may well be interesting, perhaps even spiritually uplifting; it may well, however, fall short of authentically Christian preaching.

> The Bible bears testimony primarily to what God has done, is doing, and will do. The chief task of biblical preaching is to do precisely the same.

The Bible bears testimony primarily to what God has done, is doing, and will do. The chief task of biblical preaching is to do precisely the same. The climactic questions in our series, therefore, have to do not with humanity but with God. These questions may be last in order, but they are first in importance. We ask, therefore, what God is doing in the text.

Oftentimes God is a presence in our texts, a voice speaking somehow—we dare not be overprecise—to the human characters in the Bible. "Take off your shoes!" says God to Moses in Exodus 3. "Be still and know that I am God," says that presence through the psalmist. "You shall have no other gods before me," commands the voice. "Fear not, I am with you," promises the voice. Sometimes, as in the parable of the waiting father or in the story of the Garden of Eden, God is explicitly a character in the story. More often God is there in much the same way air is present in the world in which we live—as the inescapable and necessary condition for existence. God is present in most texts in one or more ways, promising rescue or blessing, demanding obedience, threatening punishment, receiving praise.

In the New Testament, God is present in Jesus Christ and, in time, in the activity of the Holy Spirit among the disciples. The activity of Christ is essentially the same as the activity of God. The reason the church eventually formulated the doctrine of the Trinity is that Christ and the Holy Spirit do in the New Testament what God does in the Old. So the church was saying, quite consistently, in its preaching. Such it was affirming in its worship. This reality is more significant theologically than any proof text for the doctrine of the Trinity or the divinity of Jesus Christ.

> The most important task of the interpreter is to ask, "What is God doing in the text?"

The first task of the exegete, first in importance if not chronologically, is to discern an answer to this deceptively simple question: "What is God doing in the text?" This question must be answered simply and directly. Try to avoid confining your answer only to some statement that continues the sentence "God wants us to . . . " That merely shifts the attention of the preacher back to ourselves. Seek an indication of what God is doing, not what we ought to do.

The second question is just as simple, and even more difficult to answer. Make no mistake; this is the most difficult and the most important of all the questions in the series. If we do not make some attempt to answer this question, we have left the task of preparation for preaching virtually undone.

> The most difficult question for the interpreter to answer is, "Is God doing anything similar in our world?"

It is indeed a difficult task to undertake, perhaps an impossible one. It is never easy, for many reasons, to dare to say before a congregation of God's people what God is doing today. One should not, for example, simply assume that God is always doing exactly the same thing in the world at all times and in all places. Consider, if you will, Isaiah 7:1–25.[42] There the prophet Isaiah is sent with a specific word from God to King Ahaz of Judah. The prophet finds the king inspecting the waterworks of Jerusalem, a reasonable precaution since it appears that the city may have to endure a siege. The rising power in the region is certainly Assyria, an aggressive and militarily irresistible force. The Assyrians loom like a threatening cloud on the northeastern horizon of Judah. Two small nations, Syria (perhaps to avoid confusion in a sermon it would be better to use the name, Aram, as in the NRSV) and Israel, lie between Judah and the fearsome Assyrians. The kings of those two nations, Rezin and Pekah, banded together to resist the Assyrians. It appeared that they invited Judah to join the alliance, and when the latter nation refused the offer they decided to invade and place a puppet king, Ben Tabeel, on the throne of Judah.

This brings us to King Ahaz and the Jerusalem waterworks. It also brings us to the sign that God promises through Isaiah. God wishes Ahaz to resist the invaders. If he stands fast, he will be "stood fast."[43] God will be faithful to his covenant with David and will save the people if they are faithful. His will in this crisis is that they should resist. To continue the story, Ahaz declines twice to receive a sign from God, preferring rather to trust in the ways of power politics. He sends tribute to the king of Assyria and calls on him to deal with the enemies of Judah. Ahaz has more faith in the king of Assyria than in the God whom he worships in the Temple. This is not only bad theology, by the way; it is also dubious politics. It is rather like calling in the Mafia to deal with the young punks at the street corner. Isaiah, infuriated, offers the famous sign of Immanuel, "God with us." A young woman will have enough faith to call her child "Immanuel," displaying the faith Ahaz so conspicuously lacks. This is a sign that would bring salvation to one who trusts but brings only disaster to the one who refuses to believe. Perhaps one might want to think of another young woman of faith who also has a baby boy, who likewise is a sign that will cause both the fall and the rising of many in Israel (Luke 2:34–35).

All this should not obscure the fact, however, that God is promising aid and urging resistance to the foreign invader. If we were to jump forward a century and a half, however, we would find in Jeremiah, chapter 28, a prophet walking the streets of Jerusalem wearing an ox yoke as a sign that Judah must surrender to the enemy. God, declares the strange prophet, has given over the city and the people to the Babylonians. God is not defending the people but, as it were, making war against them. Another prophet, Hananiah, prophesies using the words of divine authority, "Thus says the Lord!" He predicts that the Lord will smash the yoke of the Babylonians and will rescue the people from the enemy. Perhaps Hananiah is an analogical preacher! He sees an analogy between his situation and the situation of Judah in Isaiah's time. "Trust and God will deliver you" is the message! Like prophets before him, like Jeremiah, for that matter, he adds sign to word, tears the yoke from Jeremiah's neck, and smashes it. These are the words and the actions of a true prophet, or so it seems. But if Hananiah is an analogical preacher, he is one who is insufficiently aware that the sovereign God is free to do a new thing, even a terrible new thing. The word that came through Isaiah is not the same as the word that is coming to this new situation.

Let Hananiah serve as a terrible warning to us, for he is dead wrong, and he will be punished for his presumption. It is Jeremiah who speaks the true word from God, terrible as it is. Let none of us presume that it is easy to know what God is doing in our world. It is, however, terribly easy, deadly easy, to let our wishes, our preoccupations, our ideological fixations masquerade as the word of God. Here I can give no advice; here technique must give way to trust. Here the power of the Holy Spirit alone suffices.

We are not left without clues, however. God is not arbitrary or inconsistent. We can turn to the record of God's dealing with humanity in the past and discern some patterns there. This too is a form of analogical thinking. Jeremiah himself responds to Hananiah with a pious wish that Hananiah's word may be true—"May it be so!" But he doesn't believe that it is so. It is, in part, the record of the past that persuades him otherwise: "The prophets who preceded you and me from ancient times prophesied war, famine, and pestilence against many countries and great kingdoms."

> God is not arbitrary or inconsistent. We can turn to the record of God's dealings with humanity in the past and discern some patterns there. This too is a form of analogical thinking.

We are not left totally without resources. The scriptures are, in a way, God's "track record." Between the power of the Holy Spirit and the record of God's dealing with humanity, the impossible may be done. Answer this question, but answer it *trembling!*

five

Putting the Sermon Together

Compose the sermon.

There are no "extensions" for Sunday morning. It follows Saturday with a fair degree of predictability, and no professor can grant a few extra days of preparation. It is time to compose the sermon. Many possibilities for the form of your sermon lie before you. You have brought together in your work the world of the text and the world in which you live and are ready actually to compose the sermon.

PROBLEM/RESOLUTION SERMONS

If you are or were struck largely with a problem or a difficulty, if you noticed first some difference or distance between text and your world, you might wish to try a problem/solution inductive sermon. Having such difficulties is not a sign of disloyalty to Jesus Christ, the Christian faith, or the Bible. In fact, it may be that it is by wrestling with such problems that God's word actually comes to us. If we experience a significant problem with the text, the best starting point for the sermon may be with the difficulty itself. Several key homileticians advocate varieties of this approach.[1] It is important that the problem be of considerable importance, one that would be shared widely in the congregation or in society as a whole. A problem that is obscure or particular to the preacher will not lead to a worthwhile sermon. If such a problem with the text exists, however, this form of sermon can be extraordinarily effective.

> If the encounter with the text has been dominated by a sense of difficulty or problem, a sermon that begins with the problem and moves toward a resolution may be an appropriate choice.

Note, however, that one begins with the problem—one does not end there. It is pastorally irresponsible simply to raise a problem and not to share with the congregation the resources to deal with it. Many texts raise problems of such significance, however, that no simple solution, certainly no solution that can be reached in fifteen to twenty sermonic minutes, will suffice. (It is, in fact, a problem with this style of preaching that the problem is sometimes far more convincingly set out than the solution!) It may be possible, however, to offer the people not a solution but a resolution, a way of grasping the text that allows the congregation to get on with life a little more successfully because of the encounter. To my ear the word "resolution" allows for a little more of that ambiguity that marks so much of the reality of our lives than does the word "solution."

The great advantage of preaching in this mode is that it allows the congregation to go along on the journey that the minister or priest has already undertaken. The minister or priest working on a sermon does not know from the beginning what the text or the sermon is about, but must try out various possibilities and bring to bear various pieces of information before eventually working through to a conclusion she or he can live with. In other words, the process leads toward a conclusion; it is "inductive." (Inductive comes from the Latin for "lead toward.") Most ministers find such a process genuinely interesting. They also feel a considerable level of confidence in the conclusions they are able to reach.

In traditional preaching this conclusion, reached inductively, is then used deductively, that is, as the theme that is expanded, illustrated, subdivided, and applied. Such preaching is often tedious. Why not, suggested Fred Craddock, replicate in the pulpit the process that took place in the study? Such a process would generally be more interesting to the listener, he argued. In a murder mystery the author does not usually tell us "whodunit" until very near the end of the story. Who would buy a mystery in which the murderer is identified on page one?[2] In preaching, on the other hand, we regularly tell our listeners what the sermon is about in the second paragraph!

The inductive method at its best allows the listeners to experience the process of discovery along with the preacher. Such listeners are far more likely genuinely to claim for themselves the conclusions they do eventually reach with the sermon. This process also respects the integrity and the intellectual capacities of the congregation. These are thinking, feeling, often deeply spiritual people to whom we are speaking. Even those preachers who never compose an inductive sermon in their lives ought to take with them always this attitude of respect.

There are many forms of inductive sermons, but the problem/resolution form is a relatively easy one to implement. A typical sermon might proceed like this:

Problem

Development of problem

Information and images relevant to the text

First attempt at resolution (not truly satisfying)

More information and images

Second attempt at resolution (still not satisfying)

More information and images

Resolution

The number of partial or incomplete attempts at resolution will vary from sermon to sermon. Two such attempts plus a final resolution often seems to work well, however. (Perhaps this is a homiletical hangover from the old three-point sermon days!) The information and images should not only deepen our knowledge of the text but also show why the early attempts at resolution are not truly satisfying.

A text with an obvious "problem" is Luke 16:1–9, the parable of the unjust steward. In that parable it appears that Jesus actually praises dishonesty! A problem/resolution sermon (without the information and images) on this text might flow like this:

Problem

Jesus appears to praise dishonesty

He even says the children of this age
are shrewder than the children of light

Information and images

First attempt

Perhaps he wasn't praising dishonesty —
maybe the steward was only giving up his commission

More information and images

Second attempt

Perhaps the steward was really struggling against an unjust landlord,

the representative of an oppressive system—

In such a context his dishonesty was at least acceptable

More information and images

Resolution

This is an eschatological parable. The steward really was a crook, but he seized his chance to secure his future in the narrow window of opportunity before him. Jesus presented his hearers, and us, with a narrow window of opportunity to secure our lasting future. Seize the chance!

The point is not that this is the correct interpretation of the parable, though I find it convincing. One could as easily substitute for it in this development one of the many interpretations of the passage. Such a model can, however, provide a cogent and sometimes compelling pattern for the composition of sermons.

SINGLE ANALOGY SERMONS

It may be, however, that you noticed first some continuity, some similarity between something or someone in the text and something or someone in our world. If that is the case, that similarity can serve as the analogical bridge over which the sermon can travel.

> Sometimes a single analogy can function as the sermon's bridge between the text's world and our own.

Sometimes a single point of contact or a single analogy is all that is necessary to shape your sermon. Imagine you are preaching on 1 Corinthians 1:1–17. You note that Paul is there writing to a divided church. The odds are reasonably good that you are preaching or preparing to preach to a church that, if not divided, is at least struggling with the possibility of division. It is at least the case that the congregation is part of a denomination that almost certainly is debating extraordinarily divisive issues: human sexuality, abortion, the authority of scripture, feminine imagery for God, and the like. Division in Corinth, division in the contemporary church—there is your fundamental similarity. You also note, however, that Paul does not begin by telling the Corinthians what they should do about the issues themselves; that comes much later in the letter. He begins by thanking God for what they already are in Christ. They are "the called saints." (There is no form of the verb "to be" in the Greek.) This sainthood certainly does not rest on their accomplishments; to the outside observer they seem little more than drunks and sex fiends and argumentative troublemakers. Rather, it rests on the gracious call of God, who wills to give the members of the church everything that they need. If anything, the church in Corinth is far worse in its divisions than our contemporary churches, and yet Paul gives thanks for them!

From this central point of contact, the continuing problem of division, the sermon will grow. Two different sorts of sermons suggest themselves.

In one sermon we begin with the text:

a. The church in Corinth was in deep trouble. They were bitterly divided.
b. But Paul thanked God for them.
c. They were holy and special because of God's call to them; they were saints. At this point we use our analogy as a bridge to the contemporary world.
d. We're divided too.
e. But God calls us special and holy; we are saints.
f. So I'm not going to tell you what to do this morning. I'm going to give thanks to God for you.

Another possibility is to start with the contemporary world:

a. We suffer from division in the contemporary church. Now we use analogy to bridge *back* to the text.
b. This is not a new problem. The church in Corinth was divided even more badly than our churches.
c. But Paul thanked God for them.
d. They were holy and special because of God's call to them. We then use the analogical principle to bridge forward to our world:
e. Maybe we're special and holy too because God calls us.
f. So, with all our problems, I thank God for you this morning.

Either sermon is possible. You will note that both use the same analogical bridge to move between text and world. It is just that the second option travels over the same bridge twice. In order to help the congregation to grasp the anal-

> Describe both sides of the analogy in similar terms so that the parallelism between the two is clear.

ogy, describe both sides of the analogy in *similar terms* so that the parallelism between the two is clear. Whichever side of the analogy comes first, describe the situation is such a way that the congregation will be prepared to grasp the similarity on which the analogical bridge rests. In many cases this can be done so effectively that the formal or explicit statement of the analogy is unnecessary. If you have described the situations well, you may be able to avoid statements such as "We're not so very different from the church in Corinth." Practically speaking, this means that the preacher should have the central analogy firmly in mind *before* beginning the actual composition of the sermon.

It should also be noted that the single analogy has two sides, a positive and a negative. The negative similarity lies in the fact that both the church in Corinth and the contemporary church suffer from many and various problems, especially the curse of division. The positive side of this single analogy lies in the good news that God loves the church anyway and calls it holy. There will usually be two sides to analogies between our texts and ourselves. It is probably best in the majority of sermons to proceed from the negative to the positive rather than vice versa. In this way the congregation is left with good news as the last word in their ears.

MULTIANALOGY SERMONS

Sometimes, however, one will see several points of contact between text and contemporary world. One can use these analogies as a way of giving movement and variety to the sermon and as a way of speaking an appropriately nuanced word to the people as well.

> Using more than one analogy can give movement and flow to a sermon.

It is often most interesting to work with analogies to the *negative* people or groups in or behind the text: to Simon the Pharisee in Luke 7:36–50; to the Babylonians or the hate-filled Israelites of Psalm 137. When doing so, it is important not to caricature these people. This is more than a matter of simple fairness, though that is valuable in itself. (Pharisees, after all, were very probably better people than most of us contemporary Christians.) Seek earnestly what is good or even admirable in them. They will then seem all the more human to our listeners, who will therefore be more ready to grasp the ways in which our failures are similar to their failures.

The *positive* characters, on the other hand, should not be represented with the verbal equivalent of halos. In the first place, they usually don't deserve the accolades; biblical heroes and heroines often are a pretty scaly lot. This is actually good news for contemporary Christians. If divine grace could reach a swindler like Jacob or an overconfident blowhard like Peter, it just might be able to reach us too. However, the key point is that, homiletically speaking, the positive characters should not always or even very often be treated as moral examples. "See what a wonderful, committed character Jacob (or Moses, or Mary Magdalene, or Peter) was! Go and do thou likewise." Such sermons are in grave danger of becoming tedious moralizing harangues. The positive characters are more interesting and believable if their dark sides are explored. We also might learn more from the exploration than from a simple "good example" sermon.

As an example of the multianalogy approach to the text, consider again Psalm 137. We often deal with this psalm by leaving out the ugly parts, preferring the poetry of the first six verses. "By the rivers of Babylon— there we sat down and there we wept when we remembered Zion." The murderous rage of verses 7–9 we ignore: "Happy shall they be who take your little ones and dash them against the rock!" But God's word for us is, I believe, in the brutal honesty of emotion in the psalm. If we cut it out, we also cut out God's word. We need the violence and hatred to make an honest bridge to our violent and hate-filled day.

The psalm, as we have seen, was written by and for exiles in far-off Babylon. The city of Jerusalem, the Temple of their God, their homes were destroyed by pagan Babylonians, and the singers themselves were dragged away to exile in distant Babylon. There, the captors demanded, "Sing us those blues. We love to hear you folk sing!" (Do you see how one analogy is beginning to be suggested even in this description?) The Edomites of verse 7 were the Jews' ethnic cousins who lived in what is now the south of Israel. At the point of crisis they had stood by and cheered the Babylonians on. How bitter were the memories! And so, quite naturally, "Happy shall they be who . . . " So may it be with Babylon and with the Edomites too!

We dare not forget, however, that the Bible has a center, a goal toward which it tends. For Christians the center and goal of the Bible is Jesus Christ, the Word made flesh, to whom the written word bears witness. Now, the Bible is a vast book, and in it are all kinds of materials which all must be judged in light of what Jesus is and does. It has long been taught that in the Bible the unclear must be considered in light of the clear, the peripheral in light of the central. Jesus is the Bible's clear center. All this means that we must never defend the hatred that fills Psalm 137. We do not for a moment suggest it is right, only that it is real. I would say something very much like this at the beginning of the sermon in order to give the listeners a hermeneutical orientation to the psalm.

The first analogy and the most natural one is to assume that we are like the Israelites in the psalm. They were God's people, religious folk, and so, we believe, are we. They faced great troubles in their lives, and so do we. They faced scorn from nonbelievers—well, one could go on indefinitely. We are the exiled Jews weeping by the willow trees of Babylonia.

But if that is the case we are also, at least potentially, the ones so filled with hate that something in us wants to smash the small skulls of even the babies of our enemies against the city wall. And, in the light of Jesus Christ, we cannot pretend even for a moment that this is excusable. Because religion touches something deep in the soul of humanity, it threatens always to bring out the hatred that is there also. (Where are you, Salman Rushdie?) We don't like this, but it is true for us also. We dare not indulge our capacity for hatred, or the identification with Psalm 137 will be too close for our liking.

There is another analogy here, however. Perhaps we are not the exiles, the oppressed, but the oppressors, or at least those who aid the oppressors and profit from their action. We in the so-called Christian West have been top dogs for many a generation. We have exiled many from their homes and destroyed many a city. And there are many who hate us. I must face the truth. I have two sons, in so many ways the light of my life. There are some in our world who would willingly, because of the oppressive color of my skin and even because of the faith into which they were baptized, dash their heads against a rock . . . or "necklace" them . . . or bayonet them . . . or . . .

All this might wake in me fear and fear's close cousin, hate, but there is Jesus who deals with hatred in another way. I will turn from hatred lest I find my life paralleling too exactly this psalm in any way, and perhaps in his mercy there will be an end to this endless cycle of head dashing and hatred.

In summary the sermon would look like this:

    a.   Introduction, hermeneutical orientation. The hatred is not right, but it's real.

    b.   We are like the Israelites in many ways.

    c.   We hate too.

    d.   We are also like the Babylonians.

    e.   We have done evil and are hated.

    f.   There remains another possibility open to us—to be like Christ and turn from hatred.

Here, three different analogies are possible; they become the basis for the sermon. You will note that the analogies are drawn between the historical situation *behind* the text and various realities in our world. The possible sermons from 1 Corinthians shown earlier followed the same procedure.

A multianalogy sermon can also be based on Luke 7:36–50. The exegetical basis for this work can be found on pages 88–93. In this case, however, the sermon is shaped by analogies between our world and the world *in* the text. Such a sermon might move like this:

a.   Introduction setting the scene and explaining why Jesus might be invited to dinner with a Pharisee. In many ways he was a Pharisee.

b.   We are like the forgiven woman. Like her we know, at least in theory, that we are forgiven sinners.

c.   But we don't seem to show her passionate love and joy, perhaps because we don't really see ourselves as all that bad. We don't believe we genuinely need forgiveness, so our reaction is, at least, muted.

d.   Maybe we're more like Simon. He's right about so many things—about doctrine, about the woman (she is a sinner, not just a person of low self-esteem), about what makes a person a prophet; and, most of the time, we in the church are right too.

e.   But he doesn't love, and sometimes neither do we.

f.   But then there's Jesus. He is a prophet twice over by Simon's own standards. He can look into a human heart, both the woman's heart and Simon's heart, and see what's there. He knows the truth, but he still loves. Maybe, just maybe, we can grow to be a bit more like Jesus.

The ending of this sermon is a bit difficult. There are two possibilities here, to end with a testimony to Jesus' unique status as prophet sent from God with the mandate of forgiveness, or to move to a mild and indirect exhortation to Christlikeness. The latter option would make the sermon end in a way similar to the sermon on Psalm 137.

It is widely believed that sermons should begin with a vivid introduction that grips the hearers' interest. While there is no obligation to be positively boring in the introduction, there is likewise no need to begin with a dramatic anecdote. One does occasionally come across just the right anecdote, saying, or image with which to begin a sermon, but such serendipity ought not be counted on. Many great preachers actually begin their sermons in a rather low-key manner, gently establishing a relationship with the listeners and building interest and tension only slowly. The use of a gripping anecdote may require a link to the first move of the sermon itself that may be exceedingly tenuous. The link functions almost as a second introduction in such cases. The "worst-case" scenario here is that the listeners may remember the anecdote and forget the sermon.[3] It is not always necessary to have a separate introduction to an analogical sermon. All that may be needed is simply to begin to describe whichever side of the analogy you have decided should come first. If the text is a narrative, the preacher may simply begin to retell the story itself. It is doubtful that any clever anecdote will be significantly more interesting than the actual material of the sermon itself. If the introduction is more interesting than the sermon, the problem does not lie with the introduction! Introductions are needed, however, when the preacher needs to set forth the basic hermeneutical stance of the sermon or to provide certain key items of information without which the sermon cannot be properly understood.[4]

Conclusions are probably much more important than introductions. For more than ten years I have had student evaluators in preaching class attempt to write a one-sentence summary of what they have heard in a classmate's sermon. (It ought, as you might expect, to be similar to the one-sentence summary the preacher composes beforehand.) The listeners most often write as their one-sentence summary the last important thing they have heard in the sermon. If listeners in the pews are similar to listeners in preaching class, this suggests that we ought to take great care in composing our conclusions. Any collection of sermons will demonstrate that conclusions can take a vast array of forms. If, by the way, you do come across the perfect anecdote, saying, or image, it might well be wiser to use it here than in the introduction. An analogical sermon might appropriately end, however, with a statement of the consequences for us of the last analogical movement of the sermon. This suggests that the key analogy ought to come in the climactic final position of the sermon. The final sentence should be vigorous, memorable, and fairly short. No book can teach the preacher how to compose such a sentence; it is mostly a matter of the ear. The homiletical ear, in this and other matters, can only be developed by listening to, or at least reading, good preaching.

ANALOGIES FROM THE MOVEMENT OF THE TEXT

Perhaps my favorite form of sermon is one that follows the dynamics of the text and allows the analogies to emerge as the text tells its own story. Here the analogies are drawn from characters or groups *within* the text to our own world. We have considered earlier at some length the parable of the waiting father. Here is a sermon that grew from that work. Note the shifting analogies through the sermon, and that the analogies are not to characters behind the text such as the Pharisees or members of Luke's church, but to characters within the parable itself.

THE WAITING FATHER

When I was in Sunday school I learned to call this parable the prodigal, or wasteful, son. But that isn't really a very good title. The story isn't just about that young wastrel. There are two sons in this story and two far countries, and above all there's a father, a father who waits for a much-loved son to come home.

The story begins with the father, and it's clear what we are to see here. God is like the father in this story. It does not mean that God is a man, the way I, for example, am a man, but that in the father we see something of God's own nature.

The father has two sons, and the younger one asks for his share of the estate. As a son he deserves a share of the estate, even if the asking is a little premature. We, looking back with late-twentieth-century eyes, see that he gains something else with his share of the estate. With his share of the estate comes freedom. It's not too hard to understand, perhaps particularly when we meet the older brother, why the boy might want his freedom, but even without the older brother we understand the desire to be free. Freedom, *libertad, uhuru, eleutheria,* older and younger, daughter and son—in a thousand tongues we humans cry for freedom. There's nothing surprising in that.

And the father gives the younger son his freedom. He knows that love cannot be commanded, it cannot be demanded; it can only be given. So the father, with absurd and ridiculous generosity, gives the son what he wants, the son's share of the estate . . . and his freedom.

As God gives us our freedom . . . to love or not to love.

So the son has his freedom and he makes use of it. But for some reason he can't be what he is, a son. He can't live in that relationship. He can't live in his own father's house. The story doesn't tell us why this is so, but we from our side know how such things can happen. Relationships are hard when there's not enough love, when you have to accept a love that someone else gives and you don't have enough love to give back. It's far easier to be on your own, owing nothing, and certainly not love, to anyone. It's easy to define freedom as being on your own and nothing more. Sometimes it's just easier . . . to leave.

So the boy leaves; he uses his freedom badly. And freedom misused, freedom abused, is freedom lost. He goes to a far country and wastes his money in riotous living. He pretends not to be who he is, his father's son, but only a man about town. As long as he has money he doubtless has friends, but when the money is gone, so are the friends.

He begins to find himself in want. So he attaches himself to a local landowner and he is sent out to feed the pigs—a fine fix for a good Jewish boy, to feed the pigs! He would be glad to eat the food the pigs dined on, but no one, no one would even give him that. He's worse off than even a hired servant in his father's house, and there's only one thing lower than a hired servant—a slave.

From his father's house to a pigpen.

From son to slave.

How many of God's much-loved children take their God-given treasure of freedom and use it wrongly? For some reason, and who knows that reason—there must a million of those reasons—they are unable to live in relationship with the God who made them and who loves them. They must use their freedom apart from that God. They must be on their own. But freedom abused, freedom misused, is freedom lost, and now they're little better than slaves.

> How many have ceased to be what they were made to be and
>   live in misery?
> How many are chained in obvious slavery—
>   to drugs or alcohol, or destructive sexual practices?
> Or are slaves to success and respectability and to their
>   possessions?
> They are slaves, nonetheless.
> They may have sold or given away everything that truly
>   matters to them.
> They may hold their heads high as they walk in honor, but
>   go home at night to a pigpen.
> It may cost a million, but if they are not free, if they are not
>   what God means them to be . . . it's still a pigpen. And
>   there are pigpens in every town and city.

I once preached this sermon in a small Ontario city, and a lady came up to me after the service. She said, "There are no pigpens here. There is a municipal ordinance that prohibits the keeping of livestock." But there is never a law against the kind of pigpen I mean. They're here.

So the boy is there in the pigpen, aching to feed his empty belly with the pods the pigs are eating, when "he [comes] to himself." He realizes who he is and what he has lost. He knows he is his father's son—nothing can change that—but he also knows that he has lost that status. He is no longer worthy to be called a son. It would be a definite improvement in his lot if he could go home not as a son, but as a hired servant. At least he would have something to eat!

Maybe he wasn't very sincere in this. Maybe he was truly sorry for the pain he had caused his father and even regretted the fast living. Maybe he was just hungry. We simply don't know. But the main thing was he was right. He was realistic and accurate about his situation.

And we know when we are realistic and accurate about ourselves that this is the way it is for many of us. We were created to be free daughters and sons of a loving God. Male and female, we were created by God in God's own image—that can't be changed by anything—but we have defiled that image. We are no longer worthy to be called daughters or sons of the living God.

It's like the ancient marble statue we see in the museum. Once it was the image of a hero or of a god. Over the years, it has been damaged; a drunken soldier clipped off its nose with his sword. Clumsy hands dropped it and shattered an ear; it becomes . . . damaged, and in time only the keen-eyed can see the image that once was there.

Perhaps that's the word. *Damaged.* There are a lot of damaged people in whom the image of God is barely, just barely, visible.

So the son decides to go home. And when he is still far off, his father sees him and rushes out of the house—the old man positively runs out of the house, sweeping all dignity aside—and embraces his son. The young man goes into his set speech.

"Father, I have sinned against heaven and before you; I am no longer worthy to be called your son. Treat me as one of your hired hands." The father doesn't listen to a word, doesn't say, "Let's share about this." This is no model for parenting! He calls for shoes and robe and a ring. You get the imagery?

> Slaves went barefoot but sons wore shoes.
> Slaves wore rags but sons wore robes.
> And the ring? The ring was the signet ring, the symbol of the
>   father's own authority.
> He was a son again, not a slave but a son.
> The father said it best: "He was dead and now is alive; he was
>   lost and now is found."

And there was a great party. There is good news here. Perhaps we have grown so used to it all in the church, sung so many hymns and heard so many sermons, that we don't recognize any longer the wonder and amazement of it all. There is good news here! So listen:

There is no child of God who cannot come home. There is no slavery so profound, there is no sin so vile, that God will not welcome that daughter, that son home with joy. There is no one beyond God's love!

> And if there is anyone here who knows what it is to be truly spiritually empty;
> if there is anyone who has wandered in the far country and has come back to the father's house;
> if there is anyone who can sing, "I once was lost, but now am found!"
> God bless you. For you the sermon is over. You can go home now.

Nobody is leaving. Perhaps this is because you all know it's not polite to leave partway through the service. But there may be something deeper here. Many of us feel the older brother has a raw deal in the story. We feel a sneaking sympathy with him. We look in the mirror and we feel "we're a lot like the older brother."

It's not that he is a completely likable character. He doesn't want to celebrate his brother's return. In fact, he doesn't even want to admit that the boy is his brother. "This son of yours!" he says to his father. And he's so ready to believe the worst about his own brother. "He wasted his money with prostitutes!" How does he know that? The first half of the story doesn't say how the younger brother wasted his money. But the older brother knows. Older brothers, older sisters always know these things.

But the worst thing about him is what he's done to himself. He's a son, the older son, the heir, a special, privileged position. But when his father comes to him he says, "All these years I have slaved for you!"

He has made himself a slave in his own father's house! The younger son had to go to a far country, waste all his money, and feed the pigs to turn himself into a slave, but the older son has done it in his own father's house. He's in a far country, a dim, dismal, gray far country of his own making, the kind of far country from which it is achingly hard to return.

Once again we have no idea why this should be so, but perhaps the person in the mirror can tell us at least one answer. Perhaps it is difficult for older brothers simply to accept love. Perhaps an older brother or sister may imagine that only by working and slaving can we deserve the father's love. After all, you have to work for what you get. And so we work and slave and deny ourselves this pleasure or that delight in the hope that God will love us. We work and slave and turn our Father's house into a grim, gray, dismal far country. This church, this whole world is the living God's house, and we live in it like wage slaves! We were made to be free. We were created to be daughters and sons of the living God. We were set free by Christ Jesus, and yet we make ourselves slaves, hoping by our efforts to make God love us. And all that time that love is there for us, a free and precious gift.

In this life you have to work for what you get. That's true in everything but the one thing that is most necessary to us. It's not true about love.

It's especially not true about God's love.

For make no mistake about it. The father loves the older son. He comes out of the house to him and begs him to come home, just as he did with his younger son. "Son," he says to him, "you are always with me and all that I have is yours."

Sometimes we think that God only loves the spectacular sinner, the ex-convict, the reformed drug addict, the former boozer. It's not true! There is good news here: With all our faults, with all our temptations to cut ourselves off from our sisters and brothers, with all our ability to make this world a place of slavery for ourselves and others, God still loves us. There is nothing that can stop God from loving us!

We don't know whether the older brother got over his snit and came into the party. The story simply doesn't tell us, because it's left incomplete. Perhaps that's because the story is left for us to complete. It's left to us to write the happy ending to the story when we lay aside our pride and accept the father's love and decide at last to come into the party.

Call this story "The Waiting Father." For at the end, as all through the story, there's a waiting father, a father waiting for a much-loved child to come home.

Won't you come, won't you come into the party?

NONNARRATIVE TEXTS

It is also possible to compose an analogical sermon on a nonnarrative text. The reader may wish to look back to the discussion of Psalm 137 for some indications of the way one might preach from a text that is not a narrative. That text does, however, name certain specific characters or groups and clearly presupposes a story. It might be more helpful, therefore, to present a complete sermon on a different sort of nonnarrative text, in this case 2 Corinthians 8:1–9. In nonnarrative texts it is often useful to consider *why* the text was composed. The text was composed to meet a particular need within the church of Corinth. Is there anything in the life of our church that is analogous? Is there an analogy of itch or need?

In the sermon that follows, I identify a particular need, the need to motivate Christians not only to give, but, quite simply, to keep on caring. This is the single analogy around which the sermon is shaped. Note that I go back and forth across this particular bridge several times. I also identify several strategies Paul used to accomplish his purpose, chief among them a reference to other, poorer, Christians who do care greatly and an appeal to what the Corinthians already know, the grace of our Lord Jesus Christ. The Brazilian story is an attempt to identify a contemporary analogy to the poverty-stricken Macedonians. I departed from the NRSV translation in verse 9, replacing the words "generous act" with the more traditional, more accurate, and more pleasing to the ear "grace."[5] It only remains to be said that there are a few details peculiar to the Toronto area, and that the concluding story is as accurately told as my memory will permit.

YOU KNOW . . .

At this point in his second letter to the Christians in Corinth, Paul is raising money—

> what every preacher in a congregation must do,
> what every representative of a cash-poor theological college must do,
> what every TV evangelist in white buck shoes and a three-piece suit must do,

That is what Paul is doing now; he's raising money.

Now, don't worry, I'm not raising money this morning; I haven't even brought any Knox College envelopes.

But Paul *is* raising money. So he writes the church in Corinth a letter.

Now Second Corinthians is part of the Bible for us; at least in theory we're duty-bound to pay attention to it. But when it arrived in Corinth it wasn't part of the Bible yet; it was just a letter, a letter that, among other things, asked them for money. Perhaps they weren't too happy to get a letter asking for money.

I mean, do you always like to be asked for money?

Don't you sometimes get a little tired of being asked for money? Are you always happy when yet another of those computer-generated letters for a worthy cause drops through your mail slot? You know the kind—"Dear Stephen Farris: Only you can help . . . "

Don't you get a little tired?

> And you go to work, a colleague is collecting for a child's school trip.
> You go to church, and the minister preaches yet another stewardship sermon.
> You come home and you want to relax and watch *Masterpiece Theatre,* and what do you get? A hyperanimated lady begging for more money.

You give and give and give and it never seems enough. You give and give and give and all you seem to get is another outstretched palm.

There's something called "donor fatigue," and you know all about it.

And so in the end the question is not just "Why give?" It's "Why work?" It's "Why bother?"

It's not just money; it's motivation.

So maybe they weren't delighted to be asked for money in Corinth, and Paul does seem to have to work very hard to make them want to give. It's money, yes, but it's also motivation.

Paul uses some of the techniques of modern fund-raisers. He assures the Corinthians the money will be in reliable hands. Titus will be in charge of the appeal; everybody knows Titus. He sets the Corinthians a challenge, just like on PBS. Look how generously the Macedonians have given, and everybody knows how poor they are! Oh, a little later he says he boasts about the Corinthians to the Macedonians, but the point is made, the point is made.

The one thing he does not do at this point is paint a harrowing word picture of the need for which the money is being raised. It's for the mother church in Jerusalem. There has been a famine in Palestine, and the Christians there are in need.

But he doesn't paint any word pictures of little David with his stomach distended with hunger, or of Widow Benjamin who once gave a cup of cold water to the Lord Jesus, and look how threadbare her cloak is now!

But it does matter to Paul that the Corinthians should give and give generously. It is a test, he says, of the genuineness of their faith. You see, the genuineness of their faith and the faith of all Paul's converts was in question. Paul had been preaching a gospel of free grace—the undeserved, unearned free love of God on which we may lay hold by faith in Jesus Christ. But his opponents were saying, "This isn't enough! You must be circumcised and obey the law of Israel to win God's favor. Paul isn't teaching you the full gospel!"

And perhaps, if the Corinthians don't give, if the gospel hasn't genuinely taken root in their hearts, perhaps it will seem as if those opponents are right.

So it really matters to Paul that they should give. So he reminds them:

"You know the grace of our Lord Jesus Christ, how he who was rich became poor for our sakes so that by his poverty we might become rich."

Suddenly he's not talking about drachmas and denarii anymore; he's not talking about dollars and cents.

He's talking about a figure we may have dimly glimpsed with the mind's eye,

> One who resisted the proud and lifted up the humble,
> One who cured the sick and made the blind to see,
> One who gave of himself until they laid him on a cross.

Why give? Why work? Why bother?

You already know, says Paul, you know the grace of our Lord Jesus Christ.

What do we have in the Christian faith? What do we have in the Christian faith to keep ourselves going on those cold gray days when we ask ourselves, "Why bother?"

What do we have that matters so much that we simply must pass it on to our children?

What do we have but this story of Jesus and his love!

When I was a minister in a parish church, I used to look after the junior high fellowship. I racked my brains looking for ways to keep those young teenagers interested. One Sunday evening I tried a game of Bible Trivial Pursuits with them. It was a disaster. For a game of Trivial Pursuits to work, you need to be able to answer at least some of the questions, and these Sunday-school-trained kids seemed to know nothing at all.

After a few painful minutes, I called a halt to the game and asked, "Why, after years and years of Sunday school, do you know nothing about the Bible?"

And one of them said, "Show us a video."

Well, I took her at her word and invited them to the manse the next Sunday for a video. Unfortunately, the only Bible video in our local store was *The Greatest Story Ever Told,* a sort of Cecil B. DeMille, cast of thousands, John Wayne as the centurion at the foot of the cross, Hollywood Spectacular. Now, I do believe it is the greatest story ever told, but it is not, in my opinion, the greatest movie ever made. (If you've read the book you always hate the movie!) There are four pretty good scriptwriters—Matthew, Mark, Luke, and John are their names, I believe—but Hollywood decided their story wasn't good enough. They changed it!

> It was terrible! The kids laughed and giggled;
> they played with my toddlers;
> they played with my toddlers' toys.

I fast-forwarded.

But then we came to the story of Jesus' suffering and death, and, by a mercy, Hollywood told it straight.

We watched as Jesus sat at table in an upper room with his friends and with one who would betray him.

We followed him into the garden and heard him pray in agony of spirit; we saw him betrayed . . . with a kiss.

The teenagers began to fall silent.

We witnessed the mockery of a trial, heard the lying testimony, watched the beating and torture.

The teens dropped my toddlers' toys.

We followed him through the streets of the city, saw him stumble under the weight of the cross, once, twice, and again.

They shushed away my uncomprehending toddlers.

And then they laid him on the cross and we heard the thump, thump, thump of a hammer on Roman nails.

And when he died there were tears in the eyes of those Sunday-school-hardened teenagers.

What do we have to pass on to our children?

What do we have to keep us going in the Christian faith when it would be so easy simply to stop?

What do we have, when we ask, "Why give? Why work? Why bother?"

> You know. . . . You already know. . . .
> You know the grace of our Lord Jesus Christ, how he who
> was rich for our sakes became poor so that by his poverty
> we might become rich.
> You know.

Oh, by the way, I don't know if they're still poor in Macedonia, but in the summer of '91 I was in Brazil, and they're poor there. I heard from a reliable source[6] that, by a conservative estimate, there are seven million abandoned or homeless children on the streets of Brazil's cities. Every once in a while, if they're too much trouble, people shoot some of them.

In São Paulo and in every Latin American city, there grow up on every open space what are called *favelas,* shack cities made of cardboard or tarpaper or plywood or whatever the squatters can find.

It would be dangerous for a person like me to go to a favela. Robbing me would be worth several months' income to anybody from a favela. But I and several others were taken to one favela by a man named Carlos, and with Carlos we were quite safe.

Carlos wasn't poor himself; he worked in a wire factory and earned a comfortable living. But seven years earlier he had become troubled by the fact that the children of the favela near his apartment were not hearing the stories of Jesus. So one afternoon he walked over to the favela, sat down in an open space near the creek that flows like a fetid open sewer through the favela, and began to tell stories.

And the children listened.

Then the adults started listening too. And if the adults are listening, you can't just tell Bible stories for children.

So he started a church service.

But if they're hungry, you can't just hold church services.

So he began to feed the children.

But it's much better if people help themselves rather than have others do all the work for them.

So he and his wife, Maria Josée, organized some of the women of the community to do the cooking.

But you can't fill the belly and leave the mind empty.

So they began classes for the children to help them with school.

But you can't just teach the children, if the adults are ignorant.

So they began literacy classes for the adults.

But you can't just teach people to read if they can't get a job, and in that community being able to speak some English can help you get a job.

So they began English classes.

While I was there the people of the little church were building an upper room—not for a pastor's study or a ladies parlor, or anything like that:

They were putting in a dentist's chair so that the inhabitants of the favela could have some dental care!

Well, the church folk gave us cornbread and thick, strong coffee and made us very welcome, but eventually it was time for us to return to our comfortable Western hotel.

I sat beside Carlos in his car, with an interpreter in the back seat. Carlos pulled out a photo of his family singing in church. There were

Carlos and Maria Josée, whom we had met, and their three sons, of whom he had spoken so proudly.

And there, standing in the middle of the family, was a lovely teenaged girl. I said through the interpreter, "Who is the young lady?"

For the first time the smile left Carlos's face, and he replied, "That was our daughter; she died. She wanted to be a missionary, but she died of liver disease."

What do you say when you hear a story like that? I never know what to say, so I replied, again through the interpreter, "That must have been a terrible tragedy for you and Maria Josée."

And for his reply I needed no interpretation.

"Yes," he replied, "but we are comforted. She is with Jesus."

There's something about the gospel.

There's something about the gospel that sends a man out, not once or twice, but again and again and again, into what is the worst hellhole I've ever seen on this planet.

There's something about the gospel that gives comfort and strength to a man and his wife when what to me as a parent is the worst of all human tragedies, the death of a child, happens.

There's something about the gospel.

One of the great things about traveling for the church to the poorer parts of the planet is that you meet some wonderful people. It makes you humble; they are so much better Christians than we are. I know that if, in the kingdom of heaven, I am within far shouting distance of Carlos and Maria Josée, I will be blessed indeed.

But of this I'm proud: The same gospel that gives strength and comfort to Carlos and Maria Josée is preached in our churches . . . and you know it already!

There's something about the gospel.

So when the day comes, and it will, when you ask, "Why give? Why work? Why bother?" you already know the answer.

You know the grace of our Lord Jesus Christ, how he who was rich for our sakes became poor so that by his poverty we might become rich.

You know!

A FEW CONCLUDING WORDS

In the year 1835 a young man named Adam Murray wrote home to his mother from the wilderness of Upper Canada, now Ontario. He had left his home in a stony and difficult part of New Brunswick to make his living as a schoolteacher and, perhaps, as a farmer. Young Adam had rather hoped to study for the ministry, but for some reason, perhaps financial, this proved impossible. As might be expected of such a pious young man, his letter is full of expressions of thanksgiving for the goodness of God. At considerable length he writes of the fertility of the land; anyone who wishes to work hard can prosper in the new settlements, he writes. All is not perfect, of course—times are hard and he is disappointed that his brother-in-law and traveling companion, John, had been unable to lend him $100 to buy a farm. But then he turns to what he considers the greatest blessing of all:

> We have the inestimable privilege of the preaching of the Gospel, twice every five months.

No subtle irony is intended. It is clear from the context that he is thankful that the gospel is preached as *often* as twice every five months. Amid all the difficulties of pioneer life, his greatest comfort is the preaching of the gospel. Amid all his hopes for the future his greatest joy is the preaching of the gospel. To hear the gospel preached was indeed an *inestimable privilege*.

Adam Murray never did become a minister, though his obituary notes that he became an elder in the Presbyterian Church and at his death he was widely famed for his knowledge of Calvinist theology. But his son became a minister and eventually a professor at McCormick Seminary in Chicago. By the way, the brother-in-law who could not lend the money to buy a farm was named John Farris.

Adam Murray was profoundly right. It is an inestimable privilege to hear the preaching of the gospel of Jesus Christ. But it is an even more inestimable privilege to be called to preach it.

May God grant us grace faithfully to preach that gospel.

Appendix:
On the Care and Feeding
of Sermon Manuscripts

[The following is the text of an article on the preparation of the sermon manuscript that I wrote for the journal *pmc*. It was subsequently reprinted in the Salvation Army journal, *Horizons*. The title, which appeared in neither journal, was my original choice for the essay.]

It is a serious mistake to become too anxious about the technicalities of preaching. To do so is to forget the sovereign and unpredictable role of the Holy Spirit in the proclamation of the word. But it is equally wrong to ignore those technicalities; there is a right and proper *professionalism* that belongs to the preacher's craft, a determination to do one's best, as far as is humanly possible, to make the words of the sermon as compelling and as winning as possible. Theologically speaking, this *professionalism* is that faithfulness in small things that wins the Master's word, "Well done, good and faithful servant."

Among the small things to which the preacher ought to give attention is the preparation of the sermon manuscript. Most of us find a manuscript an indispensable prop to our verbal weaknesses. Surely some attention should be paid to the task of making this prop as serviceable as possible.

For the most part we have gotten used to producing words in the blocks that we call paragraphs. Lines of type or of hand-written letters begin at the left hand margin [perhaps with a small indentation for a paragraph], march vigorously to the right hand and proceed without dallying down the page. After the first line of this route march, lines begin at the left without any reference whatsoever to the meaning of the line or to the rhythm of the language. Position on the page is determined by such extrinsic matters as width of the column and size of the type. This article is, to this point, but one of a million examples of this pattern. It works; using this pattern it is possible to cram a great deal of information into a relatively small area of paper.

But then there are those

> who do more than count their words,
> who paint with their words,
> who compose for the listener's ear,

and wish for each spoken word to carry with it

> a Creator's joy.
> Among them are the poets.
> Among them should be the preachers.

For many years some preachers have prepared their manuscripts as if they were composing blank verse. Peter Marshall, in *Mr. Jones, Meet the Master,* was but one well known example from a previous generation. There are many advantages to imitating them. The first is that it is far easier to read well or better, to speak well, using this method. With the "paragraph" model the preacher is forced to keep his or her head down an immense portion of the time simply to avoid losing one's place amidst the dense mass of words in the block before our eyes. Sometimes it is frighteningly easy to lose one's place even so. Look at the first paragraph of this article. You notice the two marked instances of the word *professionalism.* It would be very easy to lift one's eyes and leap from one occurrence of the word to the other, thus confusing both ourselves and our listeners. This error, called *homeoteleuton,* was common among the copyists of scriptural manuscripts amidst the calm of the cloister or scriptorium. How much more likely is it to happen in the tension of our pulpits!

Most of us would, I believe, be astounded if we could see how fixed is our gaze on our manuscripts. Many of my students express considerable surprise when I videotape their sermons at how much time they spend with their eyes towards the page and how little with their eyes towards their listeners. Observation does not lead me to believe that veteran preachers are significantly better than my students in this respect.

It has been shown in a number of studies that eye contact and facial expression make up a very high proportion of the communication value of human speech. We know this instinctively; none of us would buy from a used car salesman who would never meet our eyes. The preacher who buries his or her head in the manuscript simply gives away most of this communication value. The occupants of the typical pew feel this too. They believe that the preacher who speaks apparently without notes is more "sincere" than the wooden reader of a text. This belief is nonsense, of course—fluency in delivery is no guarantee of sincerity—but it is a reality. Why struggle vainly against it?

It is far better to use our pens or our typewriters or our word processors to lay out our thoughts in a manner that is at once more practical and more creative:

Divide the words on the page
　according to units of meaning
and
　according to the rhythm of the language.
Do not begin each line at the left,
　as if it were a military rank,
　　but let each thought find its own place
　　　on the page and
　　　in your speech.

Using this method also gives one the physical space on the page necessary to pay attention to the flow of language and to expression. One can write in at the appropriate places directions for pauses, either with the word "Pause" or with a number to indicate the relative length of the pause. Some use highlighters or underlining of different colours to indicate emphasis. One of my students, whose intensity in the pulpit sometimes made her look grim, from time to time drew in "smiley faces" as a reminder to smile and "extended arms" as a reminder to relax the death grip on the sides of the pulpit. Such manuscripts are far easier to follow and to speak with vigour; the eye does not need to struggle to pick out the next word or thought amidst a rush hour throng of its fellows.

But there is more to the matter than mere utility in reading the manuscript. It is better to compose from the beginning in thought and rhythmic patterns than to compose in the paragraph model and then use a word processor to break up the lines. Composing the words from the beginning according to the sense and the rhythm of our message can make our language more powerful, more balanced, more rhetorically effective. After years of consciously turning away from rhetoric, many of us are realizing again that public speech requires a beauty and a polish of language that is not necessary on the street corner, or the business letter or, indeed, in a journal article. Careful attention to the manuscript from the first moment of composition can aid in this task.

It could be argued that the time in this century when the spoken word made a life and death difference in the world as a whole was the summer of 1940. In that time it seemed that the spoken words of Winston Churchill were the only weapons left in the conflict with tyranny. William Manchester, in his recent biography, *The Last Lion: Alone,* devotes a considerable number of pages to the manner in which Churchill prepared his speeches. I noted with interest that Churchill prepared his manuscripts in this "speech form" or "psalm form" of which I have been writing. . . . It is reasonable to suppose that such habits of composition at least in part gave Churchill the sense of rhythm and parallelism that resulted in such lines as:

> Never in the field of human conflict
>> has so much been owed
>>> by so many
>>>> to so few.

It was Churchill's task to marshal his words and to send them out into battle against the enemies of his nation and of our freedom.
But it is our task to send our words
> into another battle,
>> a battle against evil and injustice,
>> against oppression and every form of idolatry.

It is our task so to order our words,
> that they become not our words only
> but also the gracious and merciful words
>> of the living God who calls us.

In this task even a manuscript is of importance!

THE STEPS: A SUMMARY

1. Identify the persons or groups in or behind your text.
2. Consider how we are like and unlike those persons or groups.
3. Decide if the text was a confirmation or a challenge to its first hearers. Determine whether the sermon should be a confirmation or a challenge to its hearers.
4. Determine what the text does. Determine whether the sermon can appropriately do the same.
5. Identify the movement of the text. Determine if the sermon may share the movement of the text.
6. Determine what God is doing in the text and, as far as it is possible, whether God is doing something similar in our world. Testify to the work of God.

Notes

CHAPTER 1. PREACHING AS CREATIVE ANALOGY

1. It sometimes seems as if many of us modern people have lost our sense of awe. At least it is rarely expressed publicly. I cannot recommend anything more highly as a restorative of lost awe than a night under the stars. Most areas have astronomy clubs or societies that hold public observing sessions. In my experience these people are more hospitable to newcomers than are church people, and would welcome your attendance.

2. Karl Barth allows no "analogy of being" between God and ourselves; Karl Barth, *The Doctrine of the Word of God, Church Dogmatics* 1.1, trans. G. T. Thomson (Edinburgh: T. & T. Clark, 1936), 279ff. God is totally other, a theological position that I as an amateur astronomer would find particularly hard to deny. We may not reason from our being to God's being. He does allow, however, an "analogy of faith." This allows us to say that relationships we experience are similar but not identical to the relationship between God and humanity and that our knowledge of God, though incomplete, is not misleading.

   Nevertheless, I am not, for the most part, trying to draw analogies in this book between God and humanity. Rather, I am attempting to find ways to perceive compelling analogies between people in the biblical world and people in our world and between what God does in the biblical world and what God may be doing in ours.

3. Literary critic Harold Bloom writes, "The meaning of a word is always another word, for words are more like other words than they can be like persons or things but . . . words are more like persons than they are like things." (Harold Bloom, *The Western Canon: The Books and School of the Ages* [New York: Riverhead Books, 1994], 60.) What I am arguing here is the converse: persons, including God, are more like words than they are like things. Hence we find in the Bible the prohibition of representing God by any graven *thing* but the practice of imaging God as speaker of a word. What is *most* like God, however, is a person, Jesus of Nazareth.

4. David Buttrick, *Homiletic: Moves and Structures* (Philadelphia: Fortress Press, 1987), 19.

5. The essentially narrative quality of the Bible is argued most extensively in Hans Frei, *The Eclipse of Biblical Narrative: A Study in Eighteenth and Nineteenth Century Hermeneutics* (New Haven and London: Yale University Press, 1974).

See also James A. Sanders, *From Sacred Story to Sacred Text: Canon as Paradigm* (Philadelphia: Fortress Press, 1987). See particularly pp. 18–21 on the unique sufficiency of story as "dynamic identity source."

6. This treatment of scripture is not substantially different from the classic statements on scripture of my own Reformed tradition. See John Calvin, *Institutes of the Christian Religion,* Book 1, chap. 7, and the Westminster Confession of Faith, Chap. I, secs. 4–5. I am not adequately familiar with the statements on scripture of other traditions to deal with them here. I do not, however, emphasize here the subsidiary argument in the Reformed tradition from the human marks of scripture, "the majesty of its parts," etc. I believe many contemporary people would not recognize much majesty in many of its parts and would feel that many of those parts are, indeed, rather problematic. The love for scripture and the awe before it that mature Christians acquire are the result of long acquaintance. The insistence of Calvin that it is God's own Spirit that enables us to hear God's word in scripture is, however, needed even more now than in the sixteenth century.

7. Sanders, *From Sacred Story to Sacred Text,* 17.

8. See Thomas G. Long, *The Witness of Preaching* (Louisville, Ky.: Westminster/John Knox Press, 1989), 9–11.

9. The Second Helvetic Confession, Chap. I. The confession continues: "Wherefore when this Word of God is now preached in the church by preachers lawfully called, we believe that the very Word of God is proclaimed, and received by the faithful; and that neither any other Word of God is to be invented nor is to be expected from heaven."

10. Quoted in Elizabeth Achtemeier, *Creative Preaching: Finding the Words* (Nashville: Abingdon Press, 1980), 13.

11. Richard N. Soulen, *Handbook of Biblical Criticism,* 2d ed. (Atlanta: John Knox Press, 1981), 17. It is precisely this emphasis on "likeness" that causes me to prefer the use of "analogy" to the use of "metaphor" in this work. In theory, any two or more entities could be brought together in a metaphor. To propose an analogy, on the other hand, requires the preacher to recognize and to enable the listeners to recognize a likeness between the two entities being compared. This requirement imposes a discipline over the process that may be absent in the use of metaphor.

12. David Buttrick, *A Captive Voice: The Liberation of Preaching* (Louisville, Ky.: Westminster John Knox Press, 1994), 77–80.

13. Sanders, *From Sacred Story to Sacred Text,* 65.

14. The word "understanding" is sometimes considered to refer to something more than a mere cognitive grasp of a concept or concepts. The word can refer to a basic way of relating to the world. If the term is defined in this way preaching does aim to inculcate something very like understanding. I am, however, using the word in its more restricted and more common sense.

15. See the wonderful title of a recent book by Walter Brueggemann, *Interpretation and Obedience: From Faithful Reading to Faithful Living* (Minneapolis: Fortress Press, 1991).

16. Buttrick, *Homiletic,* 14, and throughout the work. Buttrick might well disagree with the identification.

17. I remain extraordinarily grateful for that training. I will argue elsewhere that various forms of literary criticism can richly supplement but not replace historical-critical exegesis.

18. See especially Buttrick, *A Captive Voice;* and Edward Farley, "Preaching the Bible and Preaching the Gospel," *Theology Today* 51 (1994): 90–104, and "Toward a New Paradigm for Preaching," in *Preaching as a Theological Task: World, Gospel, Scripture: In Honor of David Buttrick,* ed. Thomas G. Long and Edward Farley (Louisville, Ky.: Westminster John Knox Press, 1996), 165–75. See the rejoinder by Ronald Allen in that same volume, "Why Preach from Passages in the Bible?" 176–88. The preacher's task, claim Buttrick and Farley, is to preach not texts, but the gospel. The argument of Buttrick and Farley is strongly worded, timely, and in some parts compelling. It may also be, particularly in Farley's case, overstated. Farley moves rather rapidly from asserting that only a fundamentalist doctrine of scripture could assert that there is a "preachable X" in every discrete unit of scripture to the argument that the whole "bridge" paradigm of moving from pericope to sermon has failed. There may not be a preachable X in every discrete unit of the Bible, particularly if one divides the units poorly and is forbidden to consider them in the context of the canon as a whole. (But why should an intelligent interpreter do either of these things?) There is, however, a preachable X in many pericopes, perhaps even the vast majority of pericopes. The evidence for the last assertion lies all around us. Many brilliant sermons have been preached, including a large number by Buttrick, from pericopes.

There is also a potential problem with the attempt to define "gospel" too distinctly from the particular texts in which it is embodied. The "gospel" is, in the work of the two scholars, in effect a summary of the biblical witness to the graciousness and justice of the God of Israel and of Jesus Christ. Most, if not all, texts in the two Testaments throw some light or contribute some nuance to our sense of that graciousness and justice, if only by way of contrast. One is tempted, moreover, to ask whether there is really a Christian gospel that is not incarnate in texts. Is there a danger in too sharp a distinction between texts and gospel of something like hermeneutical docetism?

Buttrick offers a specific example of a text that fails to contain gospel and ought not be preached: Ps. 137:9 (*A Captive Voice,* 11). I deal with this specific text at some length later in this volume. See pp. 82–88, 131. I also address the question of preaching beyond the pericope later in this work. See pp. 115–121.

Finally, while one must respect the theological acumen of Farley and the homiletical powers of Buttrick, one does fear what many preachers might do with blanket permission to ignore texts in favor of "preaching the gospel." The mind boggles when one thinks what preachers less intelligent and faithful than Buttrick and Farley might think is "gospel."

19. I did not invent the imagery. It is what was said about me by the clerk of session (chief elder) of the Presbyterian church of which I was then minister after a particularly poor sermon!

20. David Buttrick in his introduction to a recent edition of Karl Barth's *Homiletics* says that Barth in his own teaching actually denied the validity of this approach. Barth's denial of any point of contact between God and creation other than Jesus Christ meant that Barth consciously turned away from the contemporary in his

preaching. For a carefully nuanced treatment of the problem of "point of contact" in Barth's theology and its consequences for preaching, see Thomas G. Long, "And How Shall They Hear? The Listener in Contemporary Preaching," in *Listening to the Word: Studies in Honor of Fred B. Craddock,* ed. Gail O'Day and Thomas G. Long (Nashville: Abingdon Press, 1993), 167–88.

21. Mark Allan Powell, *What Is Narrative Criticism?* (Minneapolis: Fortress Press, 1990), 57–58.
22. Buttrick, *Homiletic,* 119.
23. The relevant section of the sermon may be found in Martin Luther King Jr., *A Testament of Hope: The Essential Writings of Martin Luther King, Jr.,* ed. James M. Washington (San Francisco: Harper & Row, 1986), 286.
24. Stanley Fish, *Is There a Text in This Class? The Authority of Interpretive Communities* (Cambridge, Mass., and London: Harvard University Press, 1980).
25. There is, of course, a potential and indeed actual difficulty of huge proportions here. For this method of interpretation to work most effectively there needs to be a community that actually knows the story. The reference to Joseph is now unintelligible to an enormous percentage of Americans and Canadians, simply because they do not know the story. They are far more likely to be familiar with, for example, the TV show *Seinfeld* than with the content of the Bible.
26. Gerhard von Rad, "Typological Interpretation of the Old Testament," trans. John Bright, quoted as found in *Essays on Old Testament Hermeneutics,* ed. Claus Westermann and James Luther Mays (Atlanta: John Knox Press, 1963), 17–39 (hereafter "Typological Interpretation"). Von Rad also claims that the historical-critical method is based on a form of analogical thinking. He quotes Ernst Troeltsch at length:

> The means whereby criticism is possible at all is the employment of analogy. The analogy of what takes place before our eyes . . . is the key to criticism. . . . Agreement with normal, customary, or at least repeatedly attested ways of occurrence . . . as we know them, is the mark of likelihood for occurrences which criticism can acknowledge as actually having happened. Observation of analogies between similar occurrence of the past makes it possible to ascribe to them likelihood, and to explain what is known from what is not. This almightiness of analogy, however, includes in principle the similarity of all historical events, which is, to be sure, not likeness . . . but presupposes in each instance a kernel of common similarity by virtue of which even the differences can be sympathetically grasped.

This form of analogical thinking concerns itself primarily with questions of historicity; it seeks to form a judgment about the likelihood of certain events reported in the texts under consideration actually having occurred. The direction of control is clearly from the present to the past. What actually transpires in the present, judged from a rather rationalist perspective, is the criterion for determining what may reasonably be considered to have transpired in the past. Nothing essentially dissimilar will have happened then. This is not the use of analogy I am advocating in this book!

27. In fact, Christ was "the rock"! Paul is here using the antitype to clarify the significance of the prototype, a somewhat unusual procedure, but the fact remains that he is using typology.

28. The literature that deals with the typological use of the Old Testament in the New is simply enormous. See, for example, the work of the great literary critic Northrop Frye, *The Great Code: The Bible and Literature* (Toronto: Academic Press, 1982), especially chaps. 4 and 5. It is important to stress once again that analogy is not identification, even within the Bible. "Typological interpretation is aware of the difference between the redemptive benefits of the Old Testament and those of the New" (von Rad, "Typological Interpretation," 37). Typology has been critiqued as a "halfhearted" approach to the Old Testament in that it accords value to the Old Testament as an anticipation of the New. (See Ronald J. Allen and John Holbert, *Holy Root, Holy Branches: Christian Preaching from the Old Testament* [Nashville: Abingdon Press, 1995], 24–26.) The understanding of analogy presupposed here ought to enable us to perceive relationships between figures or events in the two Testaments without denying the individual identity and value of either book. That is to say, the particularity and spiritual worth of the Old Testament type is not lost because it is seen to correspond to a New Testament antitype. The "message of the Hebrew Bible for Israel" can then be left "intact," a key point for Allen and Holbert (*Holy Root, Holy Branches,* 30). They are at this point following Walter Harrelson and Randall Falk with respect to a *negative criterion* for Christian interpretations of the Old Testament. That is to say, any use of the Old Testament by Christian interpreters who see in it prefigurations of Jesus Christ that does not allow the Hebrew scriptures to speak directly to Israel and indeed, one presumes, to any other interested group is theologically inappropriate. Typology ought not be considered in itself anti-Judaic. Note the examples of typology *within the* Older Testament!

29. See Mark Ellingsen, *The Integrity of Biblical Narrative: Story in Theology and Proclamation* (Minneapolis: Augsburg Fortress, 1990), 47–48. The standard work on the history of preaching remains Yngve Brilioth, *A Brief History of Preaching* (Philadelphia: Fortress Press, 1965) . A more contemporary but briefer work is Paul Wilson's *A Concise History of Preaching* (Nashville: Abingdon Press, 1992). This book is particularly helpful because it contains brief sections of actual sermons by the preacher being described. Another helpful work is Richard Lischer, *Theories of Preaching: Selected Readings in the Homiletical Tradition* (Durham, N.C.: Labyrinth Press, 1987).

30. See Stuart Hall, ed. and trans., *Melito of Sardis "On Pascha" and Fragments* (Oxford: Clarendon Press, 1979), 31.

31. David L. Puckett, *John Calvin's Exegesis of the Old Testament,* Columbia Series in Reformed Theology (Louisville, Ky.: Westminster John Knox Press, 1995), 68.

32. See, for example, the summary of Calvin's application of Deut. 1:19ff. to the contemporary church in T. H. L. Parker, *Calvin's Preaching* (Louisville, Ky.: Westminster/John Knox Press, 1992), 89–90.

33. As quoted in Ellingsen, *The Integrity of Biblical Narrative,* 50.

34. Ellingsen, *The Integrity of Biblical Narrative,* 48–49.

35. The sermon may be found in Thomas G. Long and Cornelius Plantinga Jr., *A Chorus of Witnesses: Model Sermons for Today's Preacher* (Grand Rapids: Wm. B. Eerdmans Publishing Co., 1994), 35–43.

36. Buttrick, *Homiletic,* 359.

37. This sermon may be found in Long and Plantinga, *A Chorus of Witnesses,* 62–70.

38. Allan Boesak, *The Finger of God: Sermons on Faith and Responsibility* (Mary-knoll, N.Y.: Orbis Books, 1982), 87–93. See also "The Reuben Option," in Allan Boesak, *Walking on Thorns: The Call to Christian Obedience* (Geneva: The World Council of Churches, 1984), 35–41.
39. Sanders, *From Sacred Story to Sacred Text,* 70. See also his work *Canon and Community* (Philadelphia: Fortress Press, 1984), 70–71.
40. See Achtemeier, *Creative Preaching: Finding the Words,* 66. See also her *Preaching from the Old Testament* (Louisville, Ky.: Westminster/John Knox Press, 1989), 58.
41. Ellingsen, *The Integrity of Biblical Narrative,* 86. Ellingsen's important treatment of the use of analogy is centered on pp. 85–89 of that work.
42. See the essay by David Greenhaw "As One with Authority: Rehabilitating Concepts for Preaching," in *Intersections: Post-Critical Studies in Preaching,* ed. Richard L. Eslinger (Grand Rapids: Wm. B. Eerdmans Publishing Co., 1994), 105–22.
43. This is the conclusion of a survey of contemporary homiletics contained in Robert Reid, David Fleer, and Jeffrey Bullock, "Preaching as the Creation of an Experience: The Not-So-Rational Revolution of the New Homiletic," *The Journal of Communication and Religion* 18 (1995): 1–9.
44. See, for example, Hans Dieter Betz, *Galatians: A Commentary on Paul's Letter to the Churches in Galatia* (Philadelphia: Fortress Press, 1979), 24. Old Testament scholars have long recognized such literary forms as the speech of a prosecuting lawyer in many of the prophetic books.

CHAPTER 2. THIS SIDE OF THE ANALOGY

1. Karl Barth, *Homiletics,* trans. Geoffrey W. Bromiley and Donald Daniels (Louisville, Ky.: Westminster/John Knox Press, 1991), 118–19. David Buttrick somewhat misrepresents Barth at this point. (See the foreword to *Homiletics,* p.9.) Barth does not dismiss the value of relevance; see the first clause of the quotation that Buttrick deletes. Nor does he state that he regretted ever having spoken of the First World War, as Buttrick claims. Rather he tells us, "I felt obliged to let this war rage on in all my sermons until finally a woman came up to me and begged me for once to talk about something else and not constantly about this terrible conflict" (p. 118). The advice that we should not harp constantly on even the most momentous contemporary issues is both theologically correct and pastorally tactful.
2. Barth, *Homiletics,* 17.
3. The quotation is from a letter to Philip Melanchthon, *Luther's Works,* Volume 48: *Letters 1,* ed. and trans. Gottfried G. Krodel (Philadelphia: Fortress Press, 1963), 282.
4. I was not surprised by these results. I tried a few other classical and biblical references on the kids. "Et tu, Brute" likewise produced only blank stares, "Horatio at the Bridge" met with some response, but "the Trojan horse" produced the story. They did not recognize "a Judas kiss" and several other biblical references. I have no reason to suppose that the general population would do any better than these

young people. The questions on the Bible in the basic version of the game Trivial Pursuits are "Who wrote the four Gospels?" and "What is the first book in the Bible?" The questions in Trivial Pursuits are supposed to be *difficult* for the majority of the population. I do not imagine that the inventors of Trivial Pursuits got to be millionaires by being stupid!

5. The verse is rendered in this way in Eugene Peterson, *The Message: New Testament with Psalms and Proverbs* (Colorado Springs: Navpress, 1993). This version is a paraphrase rather than a translation, but the substance of the passage is entirely accurately rendered here.

6. Long, *The Witness of Preaching,* 24–30.

7. Buttrick, *Homiletic,* 141–43.

8. For a careful and intelligent treatment of the problem of first-person material in the pulpit, see Richard Thulin, *The "I" of the Pulpit* (Minneapolis: Fortress Press, 1989).

9. I do not presently see why persons from different theological or social backgrounds cannot use the analogical method in preaching. Certainly Allan Boesak preached powerful analogical sermons during the time of apartheid. Boesak, *The Finger of God,* 87–93. See also Boesak, "The Reuben Option," 35–41.

For more information on various forms of contextual preaching, see Henry Mitchell, *Black Preaching: The Recovery of a Powerful Art* (Nashville: Abingdon Press, 1990); Justo L. and Catherine Gonzalez, *Liberation Preaching: The Pulpit and the Oppressed* (Nashville: Abingdon Press, 1980), reworked as *The Liberated Pulpit* (Nashville: Abingdon Press, 1994); and Christine Smith, *Weaving the Sermon: Preaching in a Feminist Perspective* (Louisville, Ky.: Westminster/John Knox Press, 1989) and *Preaching as Weeping, Confession, and Resistance: Radical Responses to Radical Evil* (Louisville, Ky.: Westminster/John Knox Press, 1992). For a spirited defense of contextual preaching, see Joseph M. Webb, "The Preacher and the Bible: In the Midst of a Revolution," *Quarterly Review,* vol. 16 (1966): 265–82. Other contextual theologies will shortly make their mark on homiletics. Some Korean students, for example, are now presently reconsidering homiletics in light of Minjung theology.

10. The myth of the impartial and totally unbiased observer of the text has long been exposed as a fraud. Its function was to give a privileged position to the presuppositions and biases of the one or ones who claimed objectivity. But before such claims to objectivity were shown to be wrong, they were shown to be impossible. See, for a classic treatment of the problem, Rudolf Bultmann, "Is Exegesis without Presuppositions Possible?" in *Existence and Faith: Shorter Writings of Rudolf Bultmann,* trans. Schubert Ogden (London: Hodder & Stoughton, 1961), 289–96. Bultmann's answer to his own question is a resounding "NO!"

CHAPTER 3. THE OTHER SIDE OF THE ANALOGY

1. See Dietrich Bonhoeffer, *Meditating on the Word* (Cambridge, Mass.: Cowley Publications, 1986), 34: "Whatever you do, do not take [for meditation] the sermon text for next Sunday."

2. See, for example, Long, *The Witness of Preaching*, 60–77; Fred Craddock, *Preaching* (Nashville: Abingdon Press, 1985), esp. 99–124; Deane A. Kemper, *Effective Preaching: A Manual for Students and Pastors* (Philadelphia: Westminster Press, 1985), 106–11; Paul Wilson, *Imagination of the Heart: New Understandings in Preaching* (Nashville: Abingdon Press, 1988), 49–85; Achtemeier, *Creative Preaching*, 44–59, and Achtemeier, *Preaching from the Old Testament*, 39–60; O. C. Edwards, *Elements of Homiletic: A Method for Preaching to Preach* (New York: Pueblo, 1982), 17–44.

3. Kemper, *Effective Preaching*, 106.

4. Long, *The Witness of Preaching*, 58.

5. C. S. Lewis, *The Screwtape Letters: Letters from a Senior to a Junior Devil* (Glasgow: Collins Fount Paperbacks, 1982), 82–83.

6. The standard work on the history of preaching remains for the present Brilioth, *A Brief History of Preaching*. For a more recent but less complete work, see Wilson, *A Concise History of Preaching*. An easily accessible resource on catecheses in the ancient church may be found in the essay by E. J. Yarnold, "Baptismal Catechesis," in C. Jones, G. Wainwright, and E. J. Yarnold, *The Study of Liturgy* (New York: Oxford University Press, 1978), 61–64.

7. See Hughes Oliphant Old, *Worship: That Is Reformed According to the Scripture*, in *Guides to the Reformed Tradition*, ed. John Leith and John Kuykendall (Atlanta: John Knox Press, 1984), 64–65. A series of doctrinal sermons on the Apostles' Creed by Helmut Thielicke was published as *I Believe: The Christian's Creed*, trans. John W. Doberstein and H. George Anderson (Philadelphia: Fortress Press, 1965).

8. It is certainly not the case that contemporary homileticians have completely ignored the need for doctrinal preaching. See Ronald J. Allen, *The Teaching Sermon* (Nashville: Abingdon Press, 1995) and William J. Carl III, *Preaching Christian Doctrine* (Philadelphia: Fortress Press, 1984).

9. Paul F. Bradshaw, *The Search for the Origins of Christian Worship: Sources and Methods for the Study of Early Liturgy* (New York: Oxford University Press, 1992), 21.

10. An introduction to Jewish worship and an estimation of its influence on Christian practices can be found in Bradshaw, The *Search for the Origins of Christian Worship*, especially the first chapter. See also William W. Simpson, *Jewish Prayer and Worship: An Introduction for Christians* (London: SCM Press, 1965).

11. Old, *Worship*, 83. Apparently Manton applied this homiletical overkill to many other chapters as well. See the chart on page 82 of *Worship*.

12. This was a favorite saying of my former colleague Stanley D. Walters, longtime professor of Old Testament language and literature in Knox College.

13. Many treatments of Gen. 2:4b—3:24 respect its unity as a narrative. One particularly good treatment of the passage can be found in Walter Vogels, *Reading and Preaching the Bible: A New Semiotic Approach* (Wilmington, Del.: Michael Glazier, 1986), 106–29.

14. Paul Scott Wilson, ed., *Word and Witness*, (New Berlin, Wis.: Liturgical Publications).

15. Some overeager advocates of lectionary preaching remind me of the old joke about liturgiologists: *Question:* What is the difference between a liturgiologist and a terrorist? *Answer:* You can negotiate with a terrorist.

16. Eugene Lowry, *Living with the Lectionary: Preaching through the Revised Common Lectionary* (Nashville: Abingdon Press, 1992). (I enjoy the apparently unintended double entendre of the title. I do think the preacher ought not "marry" the Common Lectionary, but only shack up with it.)
17. See, for example, Walter Vogels, *Reading and Preaching the Bible,* 45–47.
18. This is not an isolated incident. Very similar editing occurs in Pss. 5, 9, 117, 137, and many others. The examples could easily be multiplied. The preferred ending of Isaiah 6 is v. 8, although one may extend the reading to its conclusion on Epiphany 5 of Year C.
19. Haddon W. Robinson, *Biblical Preaching: The Development of Expository Messages* (Grand Rapids: Baker Book House, 1980). For a similar approach to the preaching task, see also James W. Cox, *Preaching: A Comprehensive Approach to the Design and Delivery of Sermons* (San Francisco: Harper & Row, 1985), esp. 77–88; John Killinger, *Fundamentals of Preaching* (Philadelphia: Fortress Press, 1985), esp. 44–50; and Paul V. Marshall, *Preaching for the Church Today: The Skills, Prayer and Art of Sermon Preparation* (New York: The Church Hymnal Corporation, 1990), esp. 81–100. Note that the authors represent quite different theological traditions.
20. On this point see in particular Thomas Long, *Preaching and the Literary Forms of the Bible* (Philadelphia: Fortress Press, 1989), and Don M. Wardlaw, ed., *Preaching Biblically: Creating Sermons in the Shape of Scripture* (Philadelphia: Westminster Press, 1983).
21. That a sermon is not an arrangement of space or of objects (structure), but an arrangement of moments in time like a plot, is a special emphasis of Eugene Lowry in *The Homiletical Plot: The Sermon as Narrative Art Form* (Atlanta: John Knox Press, 1980), and *Doing Time in the Pulpit: The Relationship between Narrative and Preaching* (Nashville: Abingdon Press, 1985).
22. On the matter of Christian preaching from the Old Testament, see in particular Allen and Holbert, *Holy Root, Holy Branches,* and Elizabeth Achtemeier, *Preaching from the Old Testament.*
23. It does not cost God little to give up a beloved Son for us! It may even help the listener to understand how Matthew pictures Jesus as repeating in his person the travails of God's people, yet without the people's unfaithfulness.
24. This is particularly the case where the text is well known, as is the case with Isa. 7:14 and Matt. 1:23, "The young woman/virgin shall conceive." To preach only on the Old Testament text in that case might seem a deliberate avoidance of a theological difficulty.
25. See my essay on this subject, "Limping Away with a Blessing: Biblical Studies and Preaching at the End of the Second Millennium," *Interpretation* 51 (1997): 358–70.
26. Hans Conzelmann, *History of Primitive Christianity,* trans. John E. Steely (Nashville: Abingdon Press, 1973), 64.
27. This is a paraphrase of a saying attributed to famous basketball coach John Wooden.
28. The *New Jerusalem Bible,* on the other hand, reads the plural here.
29. George Lindbeck, *The Nature of Doctrine: Religion and Theology in a Postliberal Age* (Philadelphia: Westminster Press, 1988).

30. When God's "weight" appeared, it was believed that all the senses, including sight, were overwhelmed. There was, therefore, associated with the appearance of God's weight a theophany, the notion of bright light or dazzling radiance.
31. See Long, *The Witness of Preaching,* 78–91.

CHAPTER 4. FROM TEXT TO SERMON: FINDING THE ANALOGIES

1. A little study of the career of Paul will hint to us that there may be in the background a shadowy group of opponents who are proclaiming "another gospel."
2. "Second law" is the meaning of the Greek word "Deuteronomy."
3. Even very good preachers sometimes appear to slip up here. See the sermon on the valley of the dry bones of Ezekiel 37 that can be found in Ellingsen, *The Integrity of Biblical Narrative,* 97–101. The text addresses an Israel whose national existence has been shaken utterly by the destruction of Jerusalem and the Babylonian exile. The people's life is all but gone; they are little more than a valley of dry, dry bones. Ellingsen moves by way of analogy to individual preachers and seminarians who feel "dried up" from time to time. The contemporary analogue is somewhat trivial compared to the situation of Israel in the text.
4. My own tendency would be to speak too often of the church.
5. Notwithstanding what I have said above, the Bible comes from a much less individualistic society or, more accurately, succession of societies, than late-twentieth-century North America. The more common of the two faults will be very likely to err on the side of individualism.
6. I preached from Psalm 137 on the first Sunday of the Gulf War in 1991. Rarely have I felt a congregation listening with the intensity of that group of Christians on that day. David Buttrick in *A Captive Voice* writes of Ps. 137:9, "Why would preachers bother to preach a baby-bashing text when they could be declaring the good news of the gospel?" My answer would be, "Because it brings us face to face with hatred, and religious hatred in particular."
7. The central thesis of Reinhold Niebuhr's classic *Moral Man and Immoral Society: A Study in Ethics and Politics* (New York and London: Charles Scribner's Sons, 1932), that it is more difficult for a large grouping, a nation, for example, to act altruistically than it is for an individual to do so, remains persuasive.
8. Is tolerance a virtue? Of course it is—when it is the real thing and not just a disguise for indifference.
9. The definition is from *The Concise Oxford English Dictionary,* 4th ed. (Oxford: Clarendon Press, 1954).
10. This is analogous to the third and principal use of the law in John Calvin. See *The Institutes of the Christian Religion* 2.7.12.
11. For an extended treatment of this point, see Long, *Preaching and the Literary Forms of the Bible.*
12. Richard Eslinger, *A New Hearing: Living Options in Homiletic Method* (Nashville: Abingdon Press, 1987), 96. This work as a whole is a particularly useful critique of propositional-discursive preaching and introduction to contemporary homiletics as a whole.
13. Long, *Preaching and the Literary Forms of the Bible,* 12.

14. Ibid., 50. See also the essays in Wardlaw, *Preaching Biblically.*
15. My Ph.D. dissertation has since been published: Stephen Farris, *The Hymns of Luke's Infancy Narrative: Their Origin, Meaning and Significance,* JSOT Supplement Series 9 (Sheffield: Academic Press, 1985).
16. Ronald J. Allen, *Preaching the Topical Sermon* (Louisville, Ky.: Westminster/John Knox Press, 1992), 31.
17. It is my intention to engage in a brief exercise in what is known as "narrative criticism." With respect to the Gospel of Luke, the chief practitioners of the kind of approach I shall adopt are C. H. Talbert and Robert Tannehill. In an early work Talbert called his method "architecture analysis" (C. H. Talbert, *Literary Patterns, Theological Themes and the Genre of Luke-Acts,* Society of Biblical Literature Monograph Series, vol. 20 [Missoula, Mont., 1974], 5–10), but he appears later to have adopted the term "genre criticism" (C. H. Talbert, *Reading Luke* [New York: Crossroads, 1982], 2). Tannehill, on the other hand, uses the more common phrase "narrative criticism" (Robert Tannehill, *The Narrative Unity of Luke-Acts* [Philadelphia: Fortress Press 1986], 1). The two scholars are very similar in their approach to Luke, however. Both authors also display a primary interest in the relationship among blocks of texts and between pericopes and the whole of the Gospel, or even of Luke-Acts. Both scholars would be very useful for the kind of preaching that considers the relationship among pericopes that I will advocate in the next section of this work. I, however, shall consider one pericope in particular, the parable of the prodigal son. It is my intention also to consider one of the concerns of "rhetorical criticism," namely, the strategy of the author with respect to the original audience. Mark Allan Powell, *What Is Narrative Criticism?* 14–15, distinguishes between narrative and rhetorical criticism at precisely this point. Rhetorical criticism considers the desired effect of the text and the strategy employed to achieve that effect with respect to the historical situation that called forth the text. Narrative criticism considers the effect of the text on an "implied reader." See also the definition of rhetorical criticism on p. 182 of Stephen D. Moore, *Literary Criticism and the Gospels: The Theoretical Challenge* (New Haven and London: Yale University Press, 1989).

    It is not my intention to present a history of interpretation of the parable or to offer a complete exegetical treatment of it. Rather, I intend to offer a brief and provisional demonstration of the use to which the preacher can put some literary-critical tools.
18. Any good commentary will make this point. A recent treatment of this point can be found in Joseph Kozar, "Absent Joy: An Investigation of the Narrative Pattern of Repetition and Variation in the Parables of Luke 15," *Toronto Journal of Theology* 8 (1992): 85–94.
19. For an extremely negative evaluation of the differences that do exist, see Susan Durber, "The Female Reader of the Parables of the Lost," *Journal for the Study of the New Testament* 45 (1992): 69–72.
20. J. A. Fitzmyer, *The Gospel According to Luke X–XXIV,* The Anchor Bible, vol. 28 A (Garden City, N.Y.: Doubleday & Co., 1985), 1084–85. Fitzmyer is here following Rudolf Bultmann in his description of the parable. Fitzmyer lists as other "twin peaks" parables: Luke 7:41–42, the two debtors, and 18:9–14, the Pharisee

and the publican; and Matt. 21:28–31, the two sons, and 25:1–13, the wise and foolish virgins. I suggest that several other parables could be added to the list.

21. See the discussion in the classic work, Joachim Jeremias, *The Parables of Jesus* (New York: Charles Scribner's Sons, 1972), 128–32. See also two excellent commentaries that review thoroughly the scholarly treatment of the parable, Fitzmyer, *The Gospel According to Luke X—XXIV*, 1083–92, and I. Howard Marshall, *The Gospel of Luke: A Commentary on the Greek Text* (Exeter: Paternoster Press, 1978), 604–13.

22. Moore, *Literary Criticism and the Gospels,* 14. The emphasis is Moore's.

23. Moore, *Literary Criticism and the Gospels,* 15.

24. Phillip Sellew, in "Interior Monologue as a Narrative Device in the Parables of Luke," *Journal of Biblical Literature* 111 (1992), downplays the significance of this phrase, suggesting that it merely serves as an introductory phrase to the interior monologue of the son. Considering that this introduces not only the monologue but one of the major movements of the parable, it seems apparent that he has underestimated the significance of the phrase.

25. Would it be possible for anyone familiar with the Hebrew Bible not to hear echoes here of another father with two sons, namely, Isaac? Would not the reader know that the older son has the higher status? It is noteworthy, however, that the older son is not rejected or given an inferior blessing, as in the Isaac story. The older brother is still a son and is in charge of all that the father has.

26. Luke Timothy Johnson, *The Gospel of Luke,* Sacra Pagina 3 (Collegeville, Minn.: The Liturgical Press, 1991), 238.

27. This point is noted in John Dominic Crossan, *In Parables: The Challenge of the Historical Jesus* (San Francisco: Harper & Row 1973), 74.

28. David A. Neale, *None but the Sinners: Religious Categories in the Gospel of Luke* (Sheffield: Academic Press, 1991), 158.

29. There is a considerable literature on the subject of possible "anti-Semitism" in Luke. (The term is surely anachronistic and should be replaced by anti-Judaic.) The more one tars Luke with this brush, the more one must be puzzled by the lack of a damning conclusion to this story. The answer is that the older brother is not primarily a figure of the Pharisees, but of Luke's church members. One might be willing to accept that Luke was to some degree anti-Judaic, but not that he was literarily incompetent.

30. The title is from Helmut Thielicke, *The Waiting Father,* trans. John W. Doberstein (New York: Harper & Brothers, 1959). The title sermon in this collection remains a masterly homiletical treatment of the parable.

31. See Dan Otto Via, *The Parables: Their Literary and Existential Dimension* (Philadelphia: Fortress Press, 1967), 166. Via is also very helpful in his identification of sin as being in "the wrong place" in the story, p. 170.

32. The complete sermon that grew from this exercise appears on pp. 135–139 of this book.

33. Perhaps this is connected to the fact that many professors of homiletics received their education in the era when a pericope-centered form of redaction criticism remained the dominant method of biblical criticism.

34. See Lowry, *Living with the Lectionary,* for an evaluation of the advantages and difficulties of lectionary-based preaching. In particular, see his critique of the lectionary's often peculiar cutting of texts, which recurs throughout pp. 37–64.

35. Carl, *Preaching Christian Doctrine,* 144–49. Another example is "Ordinary People," a sermon by William Willimon on the whole book of Ruth in William Willimon and Stanley Hauerwas, *Preaching to Strangers: Evangelism in Today's World* (Louisville, Ky.: Westminster/John Knox Press, 1992), 55–62. In an exegetical note, Willimon acknowledges the impossibility of confining himself to the announced pericope, Ruth 1:1–19a. Hauerwas disliked the sermon, but not because of the "effective text"!
36. As quoted in Parker, *Calvin's Preaching,* 82. Parker informs us (p. 81) that Calvin began the first sermon on every book in a similar manner.
37. Hugh Donnelly took this insight, I believe, from C. H. Talbert, *Reading Luke.*
38. What is true of the Gospels is also true of other parts of the scripture. In *The Art of Biblical Narrative,* 3ff., Robert Alter begins with a careful exposition of the reasons why Genesis 38, the story of Judah and Tamar, is not, as first appears to be the case, a clumsy intrusion into the midst of the Joseph cycle. He shows that this story of betrayal and sexual incontinence fits remarkably well between the story of Joseph's betrayal by his brothers and the episode of Potiphar's wife. In so doing he enriches our understanding of the whole Joseph cycle. My colleague, Professor Walters, often enriched us at Knox College with careful explanations of why psalms were placed in their particular positions in the Psalter. Nor is this beyond student capabilities. A student of mine, Phil Wilson, prepared a sermon for me on Psalm 22, noting the juxtaposition of the bitter lament of that psalm with the profound trust of Psalm 23.
39. Justo and Catherine Gonzalez, *Liberation Preaching,* 43–44.
40. Fred Craddock's sermon "The Hard Side of Epiphany" is available in the "Preaching Today" series of tapes from *Christianity Today.*
41. See, for example, the sermon "Tell Them," by Douglas Rollwage, in *New Teaching, New Preaching,* ed. Peter G. White (Toronto: United Church Publishing House, 1991), 81–85. The particular text, Deut. 6:20–25, was the clue that such a sermon was appropriate from that text. Douglas Rollwage is now my minister, and from time to time rehearses large parts of the Christian story to great effect.
42. See also the account of the reign of King Ahaz of Judah in 2 Kings 16.
43. This was the way a professor of Old Testament of my own student days, John Bright, rendered a Hebrew play on words in the original.

CHAPTER 5. PUTTING THE SERMON TOGETHER

1. See especially the groundbreaking work of Fred Craddock, *As One without Authority* (Enid, Okla.: Phillips University Press, 1971; reprinted Nashville: Abingdon Press, 1979). The preaching method of Eugene Lowry also begins with a sense of difficulty with the text. See his books *The Homiletical Plot* and *Doing Time in the Pulpit.* See also the relevant chapters in Richard Eslinger, *A New Hearing.*
2. Columbo is an exception. In those films, however, the real suspense lies in figuring out how Columbo will eventually pin the crime on the culprit, known to the viewer since the first frame of the film. It would be possible to compose a "Columbo" style sermon, in which the preacher would declare the point, proba-

bly an unlikely one, near the beginning of the sermon. The remainder of the sermon would show how the preacher arrived at this conclusion. Such a sermon would have an "inductive-like" flow. One wonders if such a sermon would be more clever than edifying, however.

3. I once was consulted by a minister who told me that he begins every sermon with a joke. I asked him why he did this, and he replied, "So they will like me"! I found this rather sad. The function of any introduction should surely be little more than to get the sermon under way.

4. A very helpful and perhaps the most extensive treatment of the problem of composing introductions may be found in Buttrick, *Homiletic,* 83–96. The following chapter of the book, on conclusions, is also helpful. See also Long, *The Witness of Preaching,* pp. 133–47 on introductions and pp. 150–55 on conclusions. Both authors consider introductions more significant than I do. A stance on these matters more similar to my own may be found in Paul S. Wilson, *The Practice of Preaching* (Nashville: Abingdon Press, 1995), 182–86.

5. The NRSV translates the same Greek word as "grace" in verse 1!

6. The statistic was from a speech given to the World Alliance of Reformed Churches Executive Committee by the Cardinal Archbishop of São Paulo.

Index of Scripture

THE OLD TESTAMENT

THE NEW TESTAMENT

EARLY CHRISTIAN WRITINGS

Index of Subjects